BUTCHERING DEER

BUTCHERING DEER

A Complete Guide from Field to Table

Peter J. Fiduccia

Skyhorse Publishing

Skyhorse Publishing books may be purchased in bulk at special discounts for sales promotion, corporate gifts, fund-raising, or educational purposes. Special editions can also be created to specifications. For details, contact the Special Sales Department, Skyhorse Publishing, 307 West 36th Street, 11th Floor, New York, NY 10018 or info@skyhorsepublishing.com.

Skyhorse® and Skyhorse Publishing® are registered trademarks of Skyhorse Publishing, Inc.®, a Delaware corporation.

Visit our website at www.skyhorsepublishing.com.

10 9 8 7 6 5 4 3 2 1

Library of Congress Cataloging-in-Publication Data is available on file.

Cover design by Tom Lau
Cover photo credit: Fiduccia Enterprises

Print ISBN: 978-1-5107-1400-7
Ebook ISBN: 978-1-5107-1404-5

Printed in China

Dedication

I dedicate this book to all hunters, the predators, who pursue wild game. They embrace the ritual instinct of the call-of-the-hunt to seek prey. No distance is too far to impede the pursuit. No weather so foul that it will bend the spirit. No obstacle is too daunting not to overcome. They hunt their game from valley to mountain top. When they encounter it—they kill it (not harvest it), stop to give thanks for it, butcher it, and eat it. In the end, the taking of wild game, the processing of the meat, and preparation and cooking of it brings them closer to nature than any conservationist, environmentalist, or preservationist can achieve and any non-hunter can even come close to understanding.

Photo credit: Kate Fiduccia.

Contents

Preface—Why Home Butchering?

An interesting aspect of learning the skills needed to butcher your own deer is that unlike a carpenter who has to throw away a piece of wood that was cut too short, a do-it-yourself butcher doesn't have to throw away a mistake. A piece of meat cut incorrectly simply ends up in another pile to be ground into burger or made into stew meat. I assure you anyone can properly learn the DIY aspects to butchering a deer or other big-game animal at home. I guarantee the skills needed to do this are not hard to acquire. With each passing year a hunter's abilities will get better and the time it takes to complete this pleasurable task becomes shorter and shorter.

With all of that said, however, the most important parts of successful butchering at home include having a comfortable and clean work area to skin and quarter a deer, the right butchering tools and other equipment, a sanitary area to butcher and shrink wrap the meat, and a freezer in good working order to store the meat. Having all these things makes the task go more quickly and easily, the result being good tasting venison that can last for a long time.

By having the elements noted above, like any DIY project that someone undertakes, in the end you'll assure yourself a more professional result. Therefore, before you decide to butcher your next deer, first remember that it requires an investment not only of time, but also of money. How much money will depend on just how well-equipped you want to be. The good thing about home butchering is that it can also be done on a very limited budget, with a very simple set of tools.

Most hunters don't *have* to home butcher their own deer. After all, there are plenty of abattoir facilities (more commonly called meat processing plants or slaughter houses) where a hunter can bring deer to get cut up and package. Today, most hunters who butcher their own deer or other big game at *home* do so because they want to. They enjoy the DIY aspect of cutting up their own meat.

Commercial Deer Processors

Another factor about home butchering deer is that many hunters who do it, do so because they either heard of, or have had a personal negative experience with, a commercial deer processor that ended either questionably or badly. Some of the complications hunters have encountered with processing plants include: high costs, deer hair in the meat, concerns that they have received less meat than they should have, facilities that are less than clean, inadequate packaging and labeling, and, most important, they don't know if the meat they got back was actually from *their* own deer.

One of the most worrisome aspects that I hear from hunters is how many of the processing plants will pile deer on top of each other either outside on the ground or on concrete floors in the plant. Both scenarios can not only contribute to unsanitary conditions leading to meat spoilage but also can lead to a crucial problem of the carcasses not being able to cool properly.

Worse yet, the concern by hunters about not getting their own deer meat back is a valid worry. Some meat processing plants (not all, but many) may lead customers to believe that the plant cuts up and processes each deer individually. In reality, most processing plants don't do that. Instead, the facility may have a routine of butchering many deer from different customers at one time. Unfortunately, this process allows them to place all similar cuts (roasts, steaks, chops, backstraps, ground and stew meat) from numerous deer into large plastic meat bins. It also means that other bins headed to the meat grinder will contain mixed meat from other deer placed into large plastic vats (tubs). The mixed meat is then dispensed and packaged into smaller portions of ground meat and given back to customers. This practice totally eliminates any possibility of a hunter getting only his or her meat back from a processing plant that employs this type of system—and some certainly do.

Furthermore, placing meat in vats and grinding it together from several deer potentially creates a more serious problem. Some of the deer killed by other hunters may not have been taken care of carefully, starting with the field-dressing stage. Or, a hunter may have allowed the deer to hang outside longer than it should have before taking it into the processing plant. Or, it may not have been handled sanitarily. These, and many other elements of how other hunters handle their deer, are all components that can lead to possible contamination problems.

That's not all there is to be worried about when you take your deer to a processing plant. I have a family member who brought a buck into a commercial processing plant. When he went to pick up his meat and antlers, he was told that "Somehow your antlers were misplaced." In the end, the antlers from his buck were never located. This is not an unusual occurrence for large deer processing facilities or even small facilities that may operate out of a garage, shed, or other building. The above incident occurred in a very large processing plant that butchers several hundred deer or more a season.

Not so surprisingly, the plant I am speaking about was under investigation by the New York State Department of Environmental Conservation (NYSDEC) for several suspected violations. One of the more flagrant violations that the plant owner was eventually charged with was not returning the right amount of meat to customers. Instead, the meat was used to make summer sausages that were sold at the plant. So, things like this do occur, and more often than they should. By the way, as of this writing this facility was fined and cannot process deer for a period of five years.

With all that said, though, I want to be *very* clear that there are many professional commercial meat plants and smaller processing facilities that butcher deer and operate clean, reliable facilities, and which *do not* fall into the categories I mentioned above. The key is, if you bring your deer to a processing plant, do your homework before taking it there.

Research has documented that the chief motivation for hunters to decide to home butcher their deer or other big game still hinges on assuring themselves that their meat will end up being of the *best quality* and that they have *total control* of how it is butchered, including keeping it contamination free. It also assures them that they will get the most efficient yield of the meat. Additionally, DIY home butchering gives you more control on how the meat looks, how it is packaged and labeled, and most important, how it will taste at the table. Plus, you'll know without a doubt that the meat is from your deer.

It's Part of the Hunt

There are many other benefits tied to butchering your own game, including the enjoyment of learning how to do it properly. After all, butchering the meat from a deer you have successfully hunted is an important *part of the entire hunt*, as significant as pre-hunt planning, along with the tactics you used to take the deer. Home butchering simply enhances the overall hunting experience. When hunters realize they have properly carried out all aspects of the hunt, from the killing of the deer, to field dressing, skinning, quartering, butchering, aging, and finally preparing a mouth-watering wild game dish for the table—it ends up being an *extremely* self-satisfying experience.

If hunters take the time to figure out the actual financial cost of the venison they kill, they may be flabbergasted to discover just how much a pound of venison actually costs. The fact is that venison is, without a doubt, the most expensive meat in the country, with its ultimate cost being many times more than any of the finest prime cuts of beef, including Wagyu beef.

This is especially true for those who travel long distances to hunt deer or other big game. Not only do they have travel expenses, which includes lodging and perhaps airfare, but there are also out-of-state license costs, outfitter fees if you hire a guide, and much more. Even hunters who stalk deer close to home encounter a sizeable financial investment.

If you plant food plots and practice quality deer management, then the cost of actually growing your deer has to be factored in too. In fact, in the entire history of hunting deer, hunters are now growing more food plots for deer than ever before. They spend money on seeds, fertilizers, lime, planting equipment, and much more. Then add in the cost of all the hunting equipment, the time invested in the hunt, and the cost of having a deer butchered at a processing plant, and the costs grow even more dramatically. So, when a lot of your expensive venison is spoiled and/or wasted through improper or even halfhearted handling (from the moment before the deer is killed and throughout the field-dressing process, to how it is hung, skinned, aged, quartered, butchered, wrapped, and frozen), it is easy to realize why it is foolish not to take the utmost care of the deer you kill and end up butchering yourself. You're eating meat that probably exceeds one hundred dollars per pound.

The Learning Curve

I'd like to add one other thought, namely that learning to properly home butcher a deer generally involves a short learning curve. This learning experience is easier to achieve than many people believe. Like any first-time DIY project, there are bound to be some mistakes made along the way, though they really aren't a big deal when you think about it. As I mentioned earlier, when an error is made when a certain section of meat is cut incorrectly, that piece can simply get tossed into the plastic bin that contains a variety of cut-up pieces of chunks of meat that are all destined to be ground meat. The old adage, "You have to eat your mistakes," definitely applies throughout the learning curve of home butchery. Remember this point: Anyone who has the *desire* to learn how to butcher a deer at home properly will ultimately achieve that goal. Again, I assure you the skills are not difficult to learn, and with each passing year you will become much better at it.

Acknowledgments

It was October 1968 and I was sitting in a subway car returning to Brooklyn from my job at First Hanover Securities in Manhattan. I picked up the *New York Daily News* and, as I always did first when I read that paper, I turned to the sport section to read the outdoor column by Jerry Kenney. That day, the column mentioned that a long-time professional meat processor, who also happened to be an avid deer hunter, was going to give a demonstration on how to field dress, skin, and butcher deer at his shop, The Starlight Meat Center in Franklin Square, Long Island, the following week. Kenney went on to say that the demonstration would be free but that "space in the shop was limited, so if you intended to go, you should plan to get there early enough to get a seat."

I stared at the clipping for several moments and then read it again. When I was finished reading it, I still couldn't believe that someone was going to field dress, skin, and butcher a deer in a local butcher shop. But I didn't overthink the oddness of it for long. As a young deer hunter, I welcomed any advice I could get, particularly if it was going to include field dressing and butchering deer. When I was in high school, my parents owned a two-family house with a store (a butcher shop) on the street level. On Thursday and Friday evenings and Saturdays all day, I worked at Louie Tomaso's Butcher Shop. My job was to quarter up whole chickens, trim pork chops, and slice and pack cold cuts. I never got the opportunity to actually butcher larger cuts of meat.

Four years had passed since I worked in the butcher shop, and I figured that going to a demo being given by a longtime experienced butcher could perhaps teach me a few things that would make field dressing a deer easier for me. And since the demo was going to be free, I decided to go.

Over the following several days I asked my hunting friends if they would be interested in going with me. But, given the fact that the demonstration was on a Friday night, boy's night out in Brooklyn, the only friend who was available to come with me was Howie Croft. The demonstration was going to begin at 7:00 p.m. and, remembering that the column had suggested people arrive in plenty of time to get a seat, we left work early. We went directly to the parking garage where I worked, across from Madison Square Garden, and got into my 1957 Chevy convertible and headed through the Midtown Tunnel toward Long Island. It was 3:30 p.m. We arrived at the butcher shop about an hour later. We were relieved to see that there were only a dozen other people waiting outside to get in which assured us that we would get seats. I parked my car and Howie and I joined the small line.

To the best of my memory (some fifty years later), by 5:00 p.m. the small line had grown to about fifty people. A mere fifteen minutes later there were about one hundred or more people, and by 6:00 p.m. there were hundreds of people in front of the store, having arrived by car, bus, and on foot. Soon after that, the police were called, "to unsnarl the traffic that had backed up for six blocks in all directions." The newspaper, *The Long Island Press*, reported that the police department later estimated that "two to three thousand hunters had to be turned away because of inadequate facilities."

Because of the incredible response and the amount of people jamming up streets and roads, the butcher who hosted the event did ten demonstrations into the wee hours of the morning. That man would turn out to be the man who, today, is somewhat overlooked and not given his full credit for being solely responsible for bringing deer hunting, and the development of countless deer hunting products, to the forefront of the entire nation. The man's name: Joe DeFalco. Within a short year or two after that evening, Joe DeFalco became a household name to an overwhelming number of deer hunters.

Shortly after the demo, thousands of people wrote to DeFalco. Many of them mentioned they were turned away from the first event. In response to the "5,600-plus letters" DeFalco received after that first event, he announced he would put on another demonstration three weeks later at a much larger venue. Incredibly, more than three thousand people jammed into the Plattduetsche Park Restaurant in Franklin Square. Joe DeFalco arrived on the hunting scene like no one else ever has. During his career, it is said that he made several million dollars from product endorsements, book sales and royalties, video sales, real estate, his own line of hunting products, including a book titled *The Complete Deer Hunt*, which was said to have sold "three and a half million copies" and a video (that's what they

were called back then), *The Hunter's Guide to Field Dressing, Skinning &
Butchering Your Deer*. This video was equally as successful as DeFalco's book.

In January 1983, *Sports Illustrated* magazine (at that time, regularly
read by more than thirty million people each week) did a six-page feature
article on Joe. It shocked the hunting world because never before, and to
my knowledge never again, did *Sports Illustrated* ever publish a feature article about a hunter or about hunting. DeFalco is responsible for countless
people becoming hunters and for educating countless hunters about field
dressing, skinning, and butchering deer properly.

While sitting in The Starlight Meat Center that evening watching Joe
DeFalco work his magic with both the audience and butchering the deer,
I would have never imagined that I would eventually make my living as
a full-time outdoor journalist and the host of a television show ("Woods
N' Water") broadcast throughout North America. When I look back, it
was only a short decade or so later that Joe and I both were members of
the same professional organizations: the Outdoor Writers Association of
America (OWAA) and the New York State Outdoor Writers Association

Photo Credit: Fiduccia Enterprises

*The author with Joe DeFalco, decades after attending DeFalco's first butchering
demonstration.*

(NYSOWA). Today, I'm grateful to say how much I admire and respect Joe DeFalco. I'm also very pleased that over the last five-plus decades Joe DeFalco and I have become friends. It was Joe's success that once played a considerable role in my aspirations to seek a full-time career in the outdoor industry.

DeFalco's amazing accomplishments were primarily due to him being the first deer hunter to tap into a market of countless hunters across the entire nation who sought information about field dressing, skinning, and butchering deer at home. It was a hot topic in 1968 and is a subject that is equally in high demand today. Thanks to Joe DeFalco, the information I have learned from his live presentations, his writings, and video productions were an impetus for my outdoor career. DeFalco was the genesis of outdoor celebrities who specialized in hunting whitetail deer. Without him, I seriously doubt that the amount of equipment to hunt whitetail deer would be where it is today. DeFalco was then, and is today, a master marketer who brought the sport of hunting whitetail deer to the forefront of millions of hunters, manufacturers, and celebrities all across North America. We all owe him a note of thanks. One way to do that would be for him to be placed in the Outdoor Writers Hall of Fame. In my mind's eye, Joe DeFalco has definitely earned that special privilege.

This book combines my own experiences over my five-plus decades of hunting, field dressing, skinning, and butchering deer, along with the knowledge of Joe DeFalco and other professional butchers who have shared their techniques with me about this subject. All have shared their knowledge and skills with me and for that I am grateful. I hope to impart to you their quality information and guidance, along with my own wide-ranging knowledge. The material within is designed to help you take your field dressing, skinning, quartering, and butchering skills to the next level.

I would like to extend my heartfelt thanks to Ted Rose, who, as always, was kind enough to allow me to use his wildlife deer photos in this book as well as others. Ted is an excellent wildlife photographer and an even better long-time friend.

People, manufacturers, and companies who provided support, knowledgeable information, butchering photos and/or images of products include Kerry Swendsen, the founder and proprietor of Deer Dummy products; John Person, a professional deer processor and the owner/operator of GameButchers, LLC: Mike Ring, a passionate buck hunter who processes deer meat in delectable smoked and other sausage and traditional cuts of venison; neighbors Darren and Devan Hazen, accomplished deer hunters, venison processors, and sausage makers; Terrence J. Daly, a professional beef and other domestic animal butcher; Richard Yvon, avid deer hunter and professional outfitter from Maine; Debbie Hall, a talented graphic artist who I have learned from and enjoyed working with for nearly two decades; Bookspan Book Clubs, Creative Publishing International; and Valerie Gleason, who has provided many photos and products over the years for many of the books both Kate and I have written. Gleason is the public relations/marketing manager for Chef's Choice by EdgeCraft Corporation.

Introduction

The most recent research by archaeologists has now emphatically documented that the first evolutionary change in the human diet combined meat and marrow. Evidence showed that, at that time, meat was mostly scavenged from large dead animals and/or occasionally obtained by hunting. What is striking about this is that it took place as early as 2.6 million years ago.

Evolutionary scientists theorize that the diet of most early hominins (a primate of a taxonomic tribe [*Hominini*], which comprises those species regarded as human, directly ancestral to humans, or very closely related to humans) was most likely very similar to the diet of modern humans' genetically closest relatives, the chimpanzees. Their diets mostly consist of fruit, but also incorporate vegetation, insects, and occasionally red meat.

Soon after that (in evolutionary time), our ancestors took their occasional meat eating to the next level. Their hunting tools improved, as did their hunting skills. This, too, was documented by researchers and archaeologists who discovered stone tools in caves at Dikika in the remote Afar region of Ethiopia. The evidence recovered demonstrated that australopithecine humans began eating meat eight hundred thousand years earlier than previously thought. These butchers used tools for butchering meat and breaking animal bones to eat the marrow. Animal bones were found at these sites, which contained corresponding cut marks on them. They first appear in the fossil record about 3.4 million years ago.

Humans have remained omnivorous since our earliest ancestors. However, their meat-eating tendencies slowly migrated from eating primarily fruit and vegetation, supplemented by some meat and marrow, to chiefly eating meat supplemented by vegetables and fruit (with the exception of those who choose to be total vegetarians). Because their tool-making made them better hunters, they were able to kill more game. In turn, they became more carnivorous as their hunting skills improved.

It is widely accepted throughout the scientific communities that eating meat by early hominins was the catalyst that eventually triggered the

credit: Pond5.

increased growth of the human brain. The resulting acquired cleverness associated from a larger brain capacity resulted in early humans ultimately developing an elevated mental prowess.

That single change in human evolution was the fundamental key element that spurred human development from being the prey of other animals, to earliest modern humans (early Homo sapiens sapiens) becoming one of the foremost hunters of big-game animals instead.

The word "veneison" began appearing in common use among Europeans in the late 1200s or early 1300s. It was derived from the Latin word *venatio*, meaning "the fruits of the hunt." For the next century there is no one particular spelling used for the word "veneison," and no specific definition attached to it. Only its pronunciation varies: uneysun, venysoun, wenysoun, venson, or vinzun.

As I will mention in an upcoming chapter, early use of the word venison was used to describe animals that included boar, hare, rabbit, or the red meat of almost any other wild animal. Records indicate that it was sometime around the 1400s that the word "venison" was gradually used to define the meat of deer.

Today, humans are at the peak of being successful big-game hunters. Some of us, however, entirely "hunt and gather" our food at the grocery store. Others also hunt and gather some food at the grocery store, but also still retain an urge spurred by a primordial inherited (genetic) instinct to hunt for wild game. Without any misgivings about social bias, they kill it, express gratefulness for taking it, butcher it, and they eat it.

Today, the quest for wild venison spurs an estimated fifteen million hunters to stalk game throughout North America. These hunters, who come from all walks of life, go with an enthusiasm that is hard to describe, which is barely understood by non-hunters, and which is completely beyond the comprehension of anti-hunters. They are motivated to go hunting even though they realize they will endure long hours in all types of weather, enduring physical aches and pains and other discomforts—all without a speck of assurance that they will bring home a deer.

Some hunters feel so strongly about their prized venison that even first-time hunters choose to take on the chore to butcher their own deer without hesitation, even though they may perceive the job to be daunting. It seems more important to a lot of today's hunters that they butcher their deer themselves because, by doing so, they have an even deeper connection to the overall hunt. Realistically, however, there are a lot of novice and seasoned veteran hunters who lack the basics of deer anatomy, butchering skills, and the self-confidence to butcher a 150-pound deer (or larger game animal) and then break the carcass down into smaller cuts of meat to be served as delicious table fare.

Within the pages of this book, I will strive to help you to learn how to butcher your deer at home. I will take you through the various, easy steps with a no-nonsense approach, and I will encourage you along the way. If you are questioning your ability to cut up a deer at home, don't. After reading this book, you will wonder what you ever worried about in the first place.

It's much easier than it appears to be. It may take you several hours to butcher and process the carcass of your first deer. With each deer you butcher, however, the time it will take to get the job done will diminish considerably until at last you'll get it done faster than you could have ever imagined.

Peter J. Fiduccia
Summer 2018

Chapter 1

Be Choosy about the Deer You Shoot

It shouldn't be surprising to anyone who hunts big game that our fore-fathers shot game strictly for survival. Being selective about the animals they killed and/or where the projectile hit the animal was understandably not their highest priority. Their main concern was to have meat on the table. While they wanted their game to taste good, once again, that wasn't their primary concern. That's not a common scenario for today's big-game hunter, however. Never before have all species of deer been more abundant than they are now. In my home state of New York, hunters annually kill an average of 250,000 deer every season. Nationwide, whitetail hunters take millions of deer each year. Additionally, never before have deer and other big game had so much quality food available to them.

Therefore, today's hunters can afford to be much more selective about the deer they shoot. Being choosy about the animal and where the shot is placed will inevitably end up providing hunters the best tasting venison. By buying this book, I surmise that you not only want to learn how to butcher your deer, but you also want your venison to taste the best it can. To accomplish this goal, hunters have to set certain considerations in their minds *prior* to the hunt. Those parameters must include selecting the right deer to kill; making sure the animal is not stressed before shooting it; and placing the projectile (broadhead or bullet) in a kill zone that will end the deer's life as quickly and humanely as possible. As any experienced hunter will affirm, the best tasting venison is going to be a *young* female deer. A close second will be an immature male deer. This is particularly the case when deer live in agricultural settings. Additionally, the meat of an *adult* female deer will almost always provide tastier meat than the meat of an adult buck. However, I would bet that most hunters go afield with a singular mindset: to shoot a buck with a good set of antlers. There are hunters, however, whose first priority is more skewed toward taking a deer that will provide good-eating meat. Fortunately, though, by simply being choosy about the consid-

Photo Credit: GameButchers, LLC.

In a majority of cases, taking a 1½- to 2 ½-year-old buck almost always assures a hunter that the venison will provide excellent tablefare.

erations mentioned above, hunters will dramatically assure themselves of better tasting wild game tablefare.

There are many reasons, some obvious and other less so, about what makes a deer taste tender. These elements include, but are not limited to, the deer's diet throughout the year, the overall health of the deer when it was killed, its age and sex, the amount of stress the deer endured prior to being killed, and whether it was in the rut (male and/or female).

Additional factors to better tasting venison include:

- Field dressing the deer quickly and correctly
- More thought to removing the deer from the woods to the game pole (i.e., not dragging the deer through mud and over other forest debris)
- Cooling the meat down as soon as possible (including removing the hide)
- Keeping the naked carcass covered in a quality game bag in order to prevent vermin infestation
- Correct butchering techniques
- Clean butchering environment
- The storage methods used (vacuum sealed and/or paper wrapped)

- Proper aging, if aged at all
- Cooking techniques

The first thing to do before taking a deer, be it doe or buck, is to evaluate the overall health of the animal. This is a rather easy thing to accomplish by quickly observing the deer. Generally speaking, by looking at the animal's overall body, one can easily determine whether or not the deer appears to be healthy. For instance, if a deer looks scrawny or small when compared to another deer, you should let it pass and look for a larger, plumper-looking animal. Again, these factors are generally more important to a hunter whose priority is taking flavorful meat than taking a buck with a large set of antlers. Taking a tender deer, therefore, is a mindset rather than a hunting objective. That's not to say that a 3½-year-old buck won't provide excellent eating. The fact is he will most often provide much more flavorful meat than a 6½-year-old buck or an old, dry doe. So, there are considerations that have to be made about the deer you are about to shoot when your overall priority is to take a deer that will provide the tastiest venison.

All the deer species (and most other wild animals) commonly go through up and down cycles of gaining and losing weight during their lives. Biologists often refer to spring/summer season, in the North, as a recovery period (from winter) for most big-game animals. Conversely, big game living in the parched regions of the Southwest or lower southern states find that period equally stressful due to the excessive high temperatures. Some deer never fully recover from these situations, while others recuperate slowly. The key point, for hunters trying to determine the health of a deer, is to realize that the present state of health of a deer is always mirrored in their coats and the shapes of their bodies. For example, if a big-game animal in the North does not recover fully during this period, its health will be reflected by the condition of its coat and its body shape during the fall.

Deer that slowly gain weight normally are obviously going to be much more flavorful and tender than deer that have not been able to recover. Like any starving animal, the instant the brain recognizes that the body is losing too much weight, it begins to use its fat reserves. In animals, the intramuscular fat is known as marbling. It's the marbling that helps to break down the muscle proteins of the meat (during cooking) to make it tender and more flavorful. Deer meat is naturally lean. So when a deer loses even a slight amount of its intramuscular fat, it affects the tenderness and flavor of the meat.

I have found the easiest way to determine if a deer is healthy is not only by the condition of its coat and muscular structure of its body, but also if it looks like a Butterball turkey. What I mean is that a healthy, well-fed deer will have distinctly round curvatures throughout its entire body. Conversely, an animal that is in poor health can display one or more of the following physical characteristics: a boney look under its hide (i.e., boney ribs and boney backbone), a significant sway in its back, a thin neck, a nose that may appear unusually long and narrow, an unusual gait, or will look anything other than fat and plump throughout its body.

Photo credit: Canstock photo.

At a quick glance it would be easy to determine this buck is in tip-top physical condition. He is stout enough throughout his body not to have lost any intramuscular fat. Choosing a buck like this to shoot will result in tender and flavorful venison on the table.

A deer's body is not the only indicator of health, however, as the antlers can also indicate whether the animal is healthy or not. Why? Simply because it is nature's way to use most of the nutrients a deer consumes to first supplement its body's growth and overall condition. Once this process has been satisfied, only then are the excess nutrients directed toward antler growth and development. Therefore, any buck that has a thick set of antlers (has some mass) rather than a spindly set of stunted antlers is a healthy animal. So it is often best, when shooting a buck, to quickly analyze whether its antlers have symmetrical main beams and good tine length. These are all good indicators that the buck you are looking at is in good physical condition. I should point out here that these attributes are found on yearling or mature whitetail bucks. So, whether the buck you are

Photo credit: Canstock photo.

This big fella is most likely 4½ years old or older. While his meat won't be as tender as that of a younger buck or doe, it doesn't mean it will be inedible by any means. If it ends up being tough, it can always be made into burger, stew, sausage, or jerky.

looking at is a 4- or a 10-point, the antlers do provide some indication to the buck's health.

One of the key factors to the development of any buck's antlers is the availability of trace mineral elements. This is why trace minerals are important to add into some food plot plantings aside from the general NPK (nitrogen, phosphorus, potassium) of a fertilizer. There are two primary groups of nutrients:

- a macro-nutrient group including nitrogen, phosphorous, potassium, calcium, magnesium, and sulfur
- a micro-nutrient group including the small or trace amounts of elements that are also important to healthy plant growth but antler growth as well. This micro-nutrient group includes iron, manganese, copper, zinc, boron, molybdenum, and chlorine.

As I have often said, this is why the soil's micro and macro elements in some areas of the country contribute significantly to producing bucks with trophy-class antlers. Other areas of the country that are lacking some or most of these nutrients in their soil are unable to produce the types of antlers that are often seen in Iowa, Kansas, Texas, and other states that regularly produce bucks with quality trophy antlers.

Because of this, you shouldn't rely heavily on judging the health of a deer from its antlers alone. There are plenty of healthy deer that don't sport large antlers because the area in which they live does not have all the micro- and macro-nutrients needed for larger antlers. With that said, if you do live in an area with nutrient-laden soils, judging a deer's antlers related to its overall health comes in to play more. In the end, just give the antlers a brief once-over and focus more on the animal's condition of its coat, muscle structure, and plumpness.

There is a lot of misinformation about what type of buck or doe to kill. Many old timers believe that killing a barren doe will provide more tender and flavorful meat than that of other deer. The conundrum here is it is nearly impossible for anyone, including a biologist, to quickly determine if a live wild doe is barren or not. The same misinformation holds true for taking mature bucks in the rut. Many of those darn old timers claim that rutting bucks are virtually inedible. To be frank, the only two male big-game animals I have ever found to be virtually inedible during their rut are caribou and pronghorn antelope. The meat from either of these two game animals is so vile during the rut that most butchers will refrain from processing the meat. Over the fifty-four-plus years I have hunted big game, despite knowing this fact, I have tried cooking the venison from these animals but have never gotten past the extremely dreadful odor from the meat as it simmered in the pan. Each time, it has been dumped into the garbage, uncooked, and taken to the landfill.

This is absolutely not the case when it comes to the meat of a whitetail buck (or doe, for that matter) in rut. While a mature 4½- to 6½-year-old whitetail will undoubtedly be tougher and less flavorful than a younger buck, just because it was in the rut doesn't mean that its

In five-plus decades of hunting deer throughout North America, I have always found that the meat from caribou or antelope killed while in rut is horrid. The odor and flavor can only be described as putrid. Other than when they are in the rut, though, their meat is tender and delicious.

meat is inedible. In the worse possible scenario, an old buck savaged by age and the chemicals running through his body during the rut can be turned into burger, stew, sausage, and jerky. In most cases, even their backstraps and tenderloins can still be tasty and tender.

Yearling deer (there are no fawns during the hunting season), which includes the season's 7-month-old deer as well as deer in their first year of life, usually weigh in at about seventy-five pounds. If you are a hunter whose goal is to get a deer with tender and tasty meat, then yearlings are the deer you want to shoot. There is absolutely no doubt they will provide top-quality venison. The key here is that their body size is so small that a shot placed in the ribcage can damage an excessive amount of meat. If you choose to shoot a yearling deer, then make sure it's close enough so you can make an accurate one-shot kill in the neck or head, which will ensure minimal damage to the meat.

All the above information is meant to provide you some clues to determining how to be selective about the deer you shoot in order to provide yourself with top-quality meat. Even this information can't supersede that fact that if the animal you shoot does not die nearly instantly, is not properly field dressed, cooled, and so on, its meat, even from a flavorful yearling, will not be at its finest. There is no getting away from the fact that some of the best tasting venison comes unaware deer that are shot and which die as quickly as possible.

Photo credit: Canstock photo.

This doe and fawn appear to be very healthy indeed. If fine-tasting venison is your primary focus, two deer like the ones pictured here should be excellent choices.

Chapter 2

Shots for Better Tasting Venison

This chapter provides information that will help hunters increase the overall quality, flavor, tenderness, and "cookability" (I made that word up) of the big-game animals they hunt. The key factor here is that this chapter was written primarily for those hunters who not only enjoy the sport of deer hunting, but also have a significant desire and keen interest in preserving and enhancing the taste of the meat of the big game animals they kill. Before going any further, a crucial point in having delectable big-game tablefare is this: a well-placed kill shot with a broadhead or bullet is the key to assuring a hunter of the best tasting meat possible. This is a comment I purposely repeat over and over again throughout this book in order to emphasize its importance to the DIY butcher.

Not all hunters eat the deer they kill. In my mind's eye there's certainly nothing wrong with that. That is, so long as the meat from their deer is given to a needy neighbor, family, or friend who enjoys eating venison, or is donated to the needy via Hunter's for the Hungry programs available nationwide. There is, however, an ever-growing number of deer hunters who are exhibiting more and more interest in not only hunting big game, but also the proper techniques of field dressing, skinning, butchering, and cooking wild game. Since you bought a book on how to butcher your deer at home, you most likely have an interest in preserving the utmost quality, flavor, tenderness, cooking methods, and recipes of the wild game meat you process.

If there is one *chief* factor that will substantially reduce the overall quality, taste, delectability, and maximum cooking potential of wild game, particularly big game (as well as all types of domestic meats), it is the amount of stress an animal undergoes leading up to its death. Animals can experience different types of stress factors including sudden tension, an instinct of ill-feeling, an instinctive perception of unease, a wariness of impending danger, and even a gut reaction of apprehension that something bad is about to happen. All these instincts lead to the animal tensing up, as they sense something is about to happen.

When that takes place, there is an immediate tightening of the animal's muscles, a significant increase in its heartbeat, with the result being that the animal's blood is quickly flooded with adrenaline. At the same time, there is a depravation of oxygen in the muscles, which allows for a buildup of lactic acid and other waste components that the deer's metabolic system cannot get rid of. The fact is, if the deer is killed during the peak of its stress response, adrenaline and all the other various chemical components and various acidic wastes will remain in the muscles.

Photo credit: Mike Ring.

To enhance the flavor of venison to its maximum level, a chief factor is to take deer that are calm and unaware of the hunter's presence just prior to the shot.

The above information includes all components that will definitely negatively affect wild game and domestic meats and impart a strong flavor, making them less than desirable to eat. This is especially true when it comes to big-game animals such as deer, moose, caribou, elk, and bear. That is why many people who eat wild game that endured a stressful demise say that the meat had a "gamey taste." On the other side of this coin, deer taken under non-stressful conditions often provide more appealing and scrumptious meat.

Other factors that contribute to poor tasting wild game include, but are not limited to, the animal not being properly field dressed, not being cooled down quickly and properly, hanging too long on a game pole, and improper butchering practices. All these elements will be covered in greater

Photo credit: Ted Rose.

One of the chief killers of fine tasting venison is the amount of stress a deer goes through just prior to being killed. Shooting a buck that is obviously stressed out means all other aspects of bringing his meat from field to table must be done correctly to preserve its tenderness and delectable taste.

depth in other chapters. This chapter primarily focuses on what a hunter can do to minimize the stress of a deer prior to it being shot.

Prior to actually shooting a deer, the one element that is often overlooked (and sometimes even purposefully ignored) by deer hunters is the extent of stress (trauma) the deer underwent preceding the instant prior to its death. The term used to describe this phenomenon by those involved in meat science is "the stress factor."

For instance, if a deer runs by your stand quickly, most likely something triggered a flight instinct in the deer. Some of the most common reasons for the deer being spooked could be from a predator pursuing it, that it was frightened (jumped) by another hunter, or one deer was chasing another. Whatever the reason, a frightened, running deer is under stress. There are many other scenarios that cause stress to a deer, but the aforementioned are probably among the most frequent situations responsible for causing stress.

The most significant type of stress is triggered when a hunter unintentionally makes a poor shot and wounds the animal, causing it to run off in an attempt to escape. From the instant the deer is wounded, its level of stress increases exponentially. This is especially true of a wound that keeps the deer alive for a long time (hours or more) before it dies or is dispatched with another shot. "The stress factor" is at its pinnacle when that occurs.

The longer a deer takes to die, the worse the meat is going to taste. That's an inescapable fact. Therefore, hunters who place a high value on ensuring they have prime tasting venison must commit to improving their shooting skills in order to *consistently* achieve a quick and humane kill with *one* well-placed shot. Killing a deer with one shot rather than two or more is obviously going to reduce the stress factor to the deer. Being able to consistently place an accurate shot in the kill-zone will help any hunter dramatically enhance the overall quality, tastiness, piquancy, and maximum cooking potential of wild game.

Not every hunter, even those that are highly skilled shooters, makes consistent one-shot kills time after time. Even the most experienced hunter will eventually make a poor shot that doesn't dispatch the game quickly and/or instantly. But please trust this: If you want more flavorful venison that the entire family will regularly enjoy and crave more of, then it is on you to become extremely proficient with your firearm and/or bow. A note here: Bowhunting equipment rarely kills a deer instantly, but can definitely kill an animal quickly enough with a well-placed shot. A big-game animal hit with a super-sharp broadhead in the right place often dies without ever realizing what just took place—thereby reducing the stress it undergoes. However, that requires a total commitment by the bowhunter to only release the bowstring when the chances of placing the broadhead in the right part of the deer's anatomy will be most successful. See the recovery tips sidebar at the end of this chapter about broadhead-hit deer. It provides recommendations on how long to wait before trailing a deer hit in different organs and so on.

In one of my books, *Shooter's Bible Guide to Whitetail Strategies*, (published by Skyhorse Publishing), there is a chapter titled "Shot Placement and Deer Anatomy Go Hand-in-Hand." The chapter provides worthwhile information on how to consistently increase your shooting skills to make one-shot kills time and again. I have included some of that chapter here as I feel it is an important element for hunters in general and particularly those hunters who process (butcher), cook, and eat the wild game they kill. I can say this about becoming a hunter who consistently makes accurate one-shot kills: It takes a commitment to practice target shooting, especially at targets that include the entire deer's body, long before the opening of each deer season. The saying "practice makes perfect" is right on target when it comes to becoming a skilled shooter.

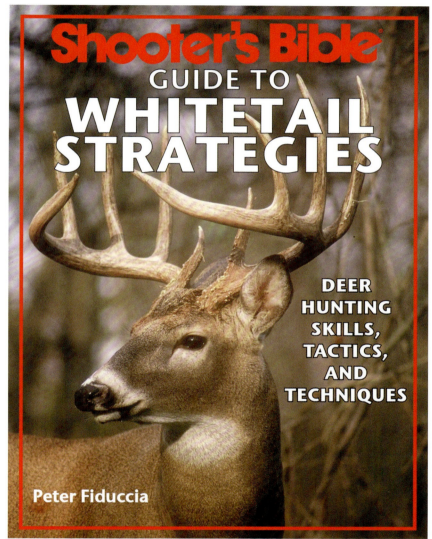

Shooter's Bible Guide to Whitetail Strategies, *published by Skyhorse Publishing, is packed with useful information. Some chapters include: How to Kill a Nocturnal Buck, Buck Core Areas, Hunt the Inside Corners, Rubs & Scrapes, By the Light of the Moon, The Rut, and much more. Available at www.deerdoctor.com and skyhorsepublishing.com.*

One other item about placing a bullet accurately and with consistency: A high-quality scope will pay off in big dividends. A riflescope does more than just magnify a deer or allow a shot in low light. It is a *very* important tool to help hunters select the exact spot on the deer where they want their projectile to impact. For instance, if you want to hit the deer each and every time in the middle of the scapula, a scope with quality glass, as well top-notch inner workings and a tough tube that will stand up in the field, will enable you to pick that exact spot quickly and confidently.

There are many quality scopes on the market today. Some manufacturers include TRACT Optics, Leica, Swarovski, Zeiss, Steiner, Leupold, Nikon, and Bushnell. When you're looking for an affordable high-quality scope, you may want to check out a company that sells their optics direct to the consumer—cutting out the markup of a middleman—and that would be TRACT Optics (www.tractoptics.com). Their line of reliable and durable high-end scopes and binoculars provide lots of value and quality that compares to the more expensive high-end models at a fraction of the cost.

Photo credit: Fiduccia Enterprises.

This is Jon LaCorte, co-founder of TRACT Optics. Jon is one of the most accurate shooters I know. That doesn't come by accident. He is diligent about practicing his shooting to keep his skills at a high level. Needless to say, he also uses high-quality scopes (in this photo the TRACT Optic TEKOA 2.5-10X42), which will aid anyone in improving their shooting skills.

Many years ago, in the mid-sixties, I was hunting on a farm in Ulster County, New York. We called the farm "Weisman's Land," after the last name of the property owner. The farm was northwest of Ellenville, New York. It was also close to a remote area known for its deer hunting and other outdoor recreational opportunities called "Big Indian Wilderness

Area," adjacent to the hamlet of Sundown. The 130-acre farm bordered several other large tracts of farmlands and woods. Weisman's property had an even mixture of an abandoned fruit orchard of apples and pears, hay fields, and mature woods. Even today, I can vividly recall every inch of the land on the farm and every deer hunt I had on it.

The one hunt that stands out in my memory was one that ended in disappointment for me, although it did teach me some very valuable lessons. As I recall, it took place in 1969 on the opening morning of New York State's regular firearm deer season. As dawn dawned (I've always wanted to write that), I was comfortably sitting on a rock ledge overlooking a large section of woods and a small pond and creek (filled with brook trout) that were about seventy-five yards below me. It was one of my favorite deer stands on Weisman's, as it rarely failed to provide deer sightings.

Around 7:15 am, I heard a deer approaching (and, now almost fifty years later, I would have trouble hearing a locomotive approaching my stand). I could tell it was alone by the distinct sounds made by the footfalls crunching leaves as it neared my stand. The deer was taking its time as it slowly walked. I got a few glimpses of it as it passed the edge of the pond through thick cover and as it continued to walk up a well-used deer trail toward me. Then the crunching of leaves stopped. For several minutes I couldn't hear the deer anymore and figured it had bedded down or quietly walked off in a different direction. Then, as most hunters have experienced, the deer suddenly appeared below the ledge without warning. I was surprised when I realized it was a really nice 8-point buck.

The buck was standing broadside about thirty-five yards away. Without hesitation, I slowly raised my rifle and was about to place the crosshairs on his chest, when he took two quick steps forward and stopped. He must have seen, heard, or sensed my movement. His entire chest area (which hunting articles in magazines from the 1960s referred to as the "boiler room" and/ or "breadbasket" for hunters to place their shot) was now hidden from my view by a large oak tree. However, I could plainly see his entire neck to almost where it met the start of his chest. Seconds seemed to tick by as slowly as minutes, and during this time, the buck turned and walked away from me downhill, never offering me a clean shot at anything other than his butt. (Later, I discovered that a shot in the deer's rear end is referred to as a "Texas heart shot".) And so, one of the largest antlered bucks I had seen on Weisman's land walked off never to be seen by me again. I can't put in print the words of frustration I muttered to myself that morning.

Photo credit: Canstock photo.

The position of this buck is close to what I saw on Weisman's land. A neck shot damages very little meat, especially the choice meat. Making the neck a prime target can be risky, however. If the projectile doesn't hit the circulatory and skeleton systems accurately, it will wound the deer—but not kill it.

As a relatively new deer hunter at that time, I didn't have much experience with deer anatomy or where to place a shot other than the chest area. At that juncture of my deer hunting, everything I had read and heard from other experienced hunters, books, and magazines touted that the only area to make a quick, clean kill was "bread basket" (the lung area). Not intimately knowing a deer's anatomy, and not understanding what other bodily areas would also result in a quick, clean kill, ended up costing me a dandy buck that day. On the trip home I made a promise to myself to learn all I could about the anatomy, circulatory system, the skeletal makeup of a white-tailed deer, and, most important, shot placement. I wanted to be sure that the next time I had an encounter like the one I had that morning, I would be able to take other shots, other than placing a shot in the "boiler room" (lungs) to kill a deer.

Between deer seasons, I started by reading everything I could possibly study on these subjects. By the time the following deer season approached I was extremely familiar with all aspects of shot placement and a deer's anatomy, circulatory system, and skeletal makeup. I diligently studied where all the organs were, the skeletal frame, and the circulatory system related to where the primary arteries and veins were. After studying the subjects, it was clear to me that instead of waiting for the buck at Weisman's farm to offer me a lung shot at thirty-five yards, I had a definite killing shot at his neck. The bullet could have hit and severed the deer's carotid artery, or jugular vein, or esophagus, trachea (windpipe), or any one of the cervical vertebrae in his neck. Any of these shots would have killed the deer in place nearly instantly. Therein lies the importance of novice (and seasoned veteran) hunters knowing all they can about a deer's anatomy when it comes to shot placement.

Interestingly, even many experienced hunters are unfamiliar with the details of deer anatomy, particularly about where to hit a deer in order to kill it cleanly and quickly. What I am about to say is *absolutely* not meant by any stretch of the imagination to sound like a brag—because it isn't. Rather, it is to substantiate that when hunters dedicate themselves to learning where to place their shots, they can learn to drop a majority of deer in their tracks.

Soon after learning all about the above subjects, I became a much more confident hunter, one who was totally self-assured when shooting deer. It has helped me to make countless one-shot kills where the deer died almost instantly. Realistically, though, not every shot a hunter takes at a deer will end that way. There isn't a hunter I know, no matter how experienced he or she might be, who hasn't wounded a deer. This will occur no matter how well-placed the shot was intended to be. Over the last fifty-five years, I have wounded few deer from shots that didn't end up where I intended them to hit.

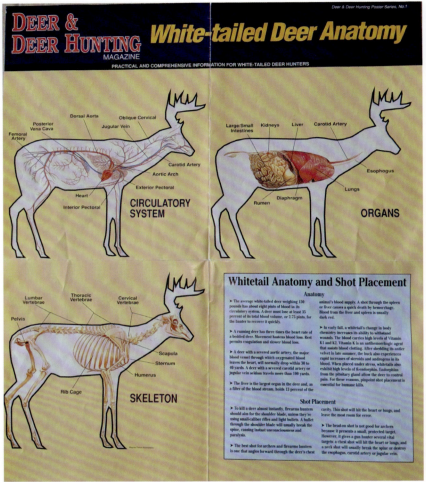

It is essential to be completely familiar with a deer's anatomy for hunters to make quick, clean, one-shot kills. Deer and Deer Hunting *magazine offers informative posters on this subject. www.shopdeerhunting.com/deer-and-deer-hunting-shot-placement-poster.*

One of the best areas to aim at for consistent one-shot kills is the shoulder blade. In fact, I have found it to be the most *lethal* area to shoot at on *any* big-game animal. To date, I would estimate I shoot at the shoulder blade 95 percent of the time. The shoulder shot has resulted in those animals falling in their tracks or within a few yards of where they were standing. I will touch on that in more detail soon. If you go to our

YouTube channel ("Peter Fiduccia Woods N' Water"), click on one-shot kills to see how well shoulder shots and other well-placed shots work to quickly kill deer and other big game.

Where Should You Aim?

Talk to any old-timer about the best shot to take at a deer and he will inevitably say "shoot for breadbasket," referring to the heart or lung areas. But in my five-plus decades of hunting big-game, I can categorically say I have much better success killing deer quickly, humanely, and without having to track a wounded animal by shooting the scapula (and, on occasion, the neck and brain), thereby collapsing the nervous system, cardiovascular system, or skeletal system (the spine). Below is some food (literally) for thought about shot placement.

The Big Five Positions

Each position a deer is in will offer various targets, including the organs, arteries, and skeletal system. The five most common positions where hunters take shots include, but are not limited to:

1. The standing broadside shot
2. The standing head–on shot
3. The standing quartering away shot
4. The standing quartering toward the hunter shot
5. The infamous, standing away shot.

> **Note:** I was careful to mention that in each position the quarry was *standing*, not walking, trotting, and/or *especially running*.

Shooting at moving deer, whether they are walking fast, trotting, or running hard is never a good idea when it comes to accurate shot placement. I learned that twice the hard way in my first year of hunting. Luckily, I didn't hit either buck, but the negative outcome of shooting at moving deer was imprinted in my brain.

From that point on I have only shot at two bucks that were running (flat out, might I add). Both ended up wounded. One buck was recovered after searching for him for several hours. He was neatly tucked into a bunch of undergrowth and brush where he had laid down. We found him only because we could smell a foul odor coming from him. Judging by the wound and the dark, almost black color of the blood, I was pretty sure I hit him in the liver (which we confirmed after field dressing him). The odor of the buck after we field dressed him was much worse than when we located him. I was sure the meat wasn't going to be the type of venison we like to eat. The outfitter, however, was more than pleased to take the meat. The buck was a huge non-typical that scored 208 B&C inches. Even though I thought I led the buck enough, my bullet hit him in the liver as he chased a doe across an open field in Saskatchewan, Canada (you may have seen that show on Woods N Water TV).

I shot the second hard-running buck while hunting on our farm in 2015. On opening day of the regular firearm season, I was in a lot of pain from a knee that had to be replaced. I planned to meet our son, Cody, by his stand at noon. Rather than walk, I drove my Arctic Cat RTV to meet him. I intended to stop about one hundred yards shy of where Cody was hunting and slowly approach his location on foot from there.

As I stopped the RTV, a doe stood up about fifty yards from me. I could see a large set of antlers of a buck that was still bedded down in blow downs near her. As I slowly and carefully stepped out of the RTV, I chambered a round as quietly as possible. The slight sound it made was enough to spook the doe and she bolted off like she was on fire. One of the largest

Photo credit: Fiduccia Enterprises.

I was lucky to find this buck. Liver-shot deer can travel long distances before lying down and eventually succumbing to their wounds.

antlered bucks I have seen on our land got up and, in what seemed like one fluid motion, ran flat-out. I instinctively raised my rifle, led the buck several feet ahead of his shoulder, and fired.

We tracked the buck for about thirty minutes before he crossed our border and went on to the land of a non-hunting neighbor who doesn't allow us to be on the property—not even to track a wounded deer. From the blood and tracks we found, it was evident that while I hit the buck, the shot was not a fatal one. In fact, at the time we thought the shot caused a superficial wound that perhaps hit the buck in the brisket. From that day on and for months later, we never heard a word from any of the neighbors or hunting clubs that someone shot a large-racked buck with a wound to his brisket or shoulder area.

One year later, on the last day of the 2016 muzzleloading season (which ended all our deer seasons), I was sitting in a blind called "Behind the Barn." Around 4:00 pm, I saw a big doe step out of the pines and begin to walk north toward one of our food plots. Within a minute, I saw a large, heavy-antlered buck come out of the pines and start to follow the doe. Both deer walked along the edge of our big swamp and kept the pines within a single jump of where they walked. The doe was walking briskly; the buck, however, was about twenty yards behind her and was walking somewhat slower. He appeared to have a slight limp. I didn't give it much thought at the time, as both deer were walking in water at the edge of the swamp and I thought his leg might be slightly sinking into the mud. The doe passed an old, but huge, abandoned beaver house we use as a distance marker. (It is exactly 162 yards from the east window of the blind.) As the buck reached that spot, I called to him using a social snort vocalization. The sound stopped him in his tracks and he looked in my direction.

I had a perfect broadside shot at a standing buck. I placed the crosshairs on his shoulder and squeezed off the shot. I could hear the heavy 295-grain bullet hit him. Even through the smoke from the muzzleloader, I could see the buck stumble forward and fall dead. He didn't go more than five yards from where he was standing, and that was only due to his momentum from stumbling forward.

The next day we skinned the buck (or as some hunters like to say, "we skun him out"—that's something else I have always wanted to write) and began butchering him. When we got to the right front shoulder, the same shoulder I shot at the buck I wounded a year earlier, we noticed something. To our surprise, we found a spent bullet lodged within the bottom of his shoulder bone just above where it meets the humerus bone. After some thought, we were all sure this was the same buck I shot and wounded a year earlier. Evidently, my shot was lower than the spot on the scapula that I normally aim at (which is in the center of the shoulder blade).

The ammunition I shot that day was a 150-grain Winchester Fail-Safe bullet. The spent load appeared to be large enough to suggest it was the same bullet. The buck's antlers were unusually heavy and somewhat gnarly looking. This was the second indication that his rack grew back abnormally, perhaps due to a prior injury that occurred the preceding year. Now his limp made sense. The wound from the previous season probably never healed fully and the buck was destined to limp on that leg the rest of his life.

Photo credit: Fiduccia Enterprises.

This is the spent bullet we found lodged low in the buck's shoulder.

I got lucky on the two running bucks that I shot at, as I found both. I lost the meat on one, however. The second buck and I had what I believe to be a meeting of destiny. This time, though, he would be standing still. Hunters will not only increase their kill ratios dramatically by shooting at standing game, they will exponentially enhance the quality, zest, tenderness, and cookability (there's that word again) of the big-game animals they hunt. *I strongly advise hunters not shoot at running bucks.* Most times it will turn out a lot worse than the two running bucks I shot at. More than that, you could wind up killing the buck but never finding it. Or, worse yet, cause unnecessary suffering to an animal—which no hunter wants to do. Lastly, if you do kill it, the stress factor will certainly lessen the overall eating quality of the deer.

Standing Broadside

By now you realize that this position is my absolute favorite position to shoot any big-game animal. It offers an ideal scenario, as you can see all the areas that can result in quick clean kills, particularly the shoulder blade (scapula). The shoulder provides hunters with the minimum amount of depth of flesh to penetrate before hitting vital areas. It is also the best position to allow hunters to mentally visualize where all the organs and other vital areas are. Additionally, no other of the five standing deer positions presents as large a percentage of body area as a target. It pays to repeat here that a standing deer (or other game)

Photo credit: P. Cody Fiduccia.

This is the buck I shot in 2016. The round tips and extra mass on this buck's antlers may be indicative of the wound from the previous year.

Photo credit: Canstock photo.

This relaxed standing broadside buck offers everything a hunter hopes to see before pulling the trigger. More important, all his vitals are clearly visible. One accurate shot through his shoulder will kill the deer almost instantly.

increases a hunter's accuracy and kill-success ratio to the *"nth degree."* (The use of *nth* means "the utmost, as much or as far as possible, to the maximum amount"—as in, they'd learned about shot placement to the nth degree. The expression derives from mathematics, where the *nth* means "to any required power," *n* standing for any number. It was first used in 1852).

Standing Head On

This is a position that only experienced hunters with good shooting skills should consider taking. There is no doubt in my mind that it is more than an adequate shot for all hunters in general. But because it doesn't provide a large target area, hunters must be sure to know a deer's anatomy well or this shot may not be for them. If a deer is hit correctly, however, it is a lethal shot. When hit properly the deer will drop in its tracks. I have killed a few bull moose in this position. All of them have dropped where they stood. Because most of the moose I shot were responding to a cow call, they usually showed up facing me. When shooting deer (or any large game) in this position, it pays to use a bullet with a minimum 150- to 180-grain load. This enables the bullet to get as much penetration as possible. When hunting moose and/or elk, I use a .270 WSM or a .308 with 150-grain

Photo credit: Canstock photo.

The position of this deer offers only one possible shot, the neck. While it isn't the best of positions to shoot a deer, it is a lethal shot if the projectile finds its target accurately. Hunters taking this shot should have a lot of shooting experience.

Winchester ammunition for both—the same calibers and ammunition I use for deer. Why did I mention this here? Because killing a deer, especially a moose or elk, isn't about using a heavy caliber rifle and load. You can take that fact to the deer hunting bank. Making consistent one-shot quick and humane kills is *always* about accurate shot placement.

In the end, I recommend this position only to those hunters who have years of shooting experience. For a majority of hunters, especially novices, this position can be a tricky shot at best. All the vital areas are much less visible. If you are not sure about shooting a deer in this position, do not take the shot. Making an accurate shot when a deer is standing in this position should be left only to those who practice their shooting regularly and have prior experiences shooting deer in this position. With all that said, this is a deadly shot and will quickly dispatch the deer if the shot is made accurately.

The Standing Quartering Away

Photo credit: Canstock photo.

While some quartering-away deer offer some visibility of the vital areas, most do not. This is a buck I would wait to shoot until he presented a much better position.

This shot drastically reduces the visibility of vital areas. The largest area offered in this position is concentrated around the digestive system (stomach and intestines). While the bullet can reach the vital areas, including the lungs, heart, and primary arteries, it will also do a lot of damage to the intestines and stomach, leaving the rumen and stomach guts in an undesirable mix of stew that will end up ruining a large portion of the meat. If the bullet only hits the stomach, you now have a gut-shot deer to deal with. It is true that gut-shot deer die. However, they can live twelve or more hours before they do and the stomach contents will either ruin the flavor of meat or totally contaminate it. This shot is best left to those who *rarely* miss what they're aiming at and who know and accept the consequences of not making the shot correctly. I don't shoot deer or other game in a going-away position and I highly recommend that other hunters do the same.

The Standing Quartering Toward the Hunter

This position is an okay position to take a shot, but not one that offers excellent shot placement. It is rated by many experienced hunters as a "satisfactory" shot to take. I would recommend that it is not a shot for

Photo credit: Canstock photo.

Only if the projectile is well-placed will this position result in it hitting the vitals and end in a successful hunt.

small calibers, however. I would suggest that nothing less than a .270, and preferably a .270 WSM caliber should be used with a minimum bullet of 150 grains. It is also advisable that a deer in this position should be relatively close range, no further than 100 yards at best and, more appropriately, no more than 75 yards away. If the shot is placed perfectly, the bullet will hit the vitals, and the shoulder blade and the animal should fall in its tracks or very close by. Otherwise, it isn't going to be an instant kill shot, but it will be lethal.

The Going-Away Shot (a.k.a. the "Texas Heart Shot")

I strongly feel this is a shot that should NOT be taken mostly because it destroys so much meat. And, if you are butchering your deer at home, it is probably because you highly value the meat of your game. So, this is not a shot for you. First off, a caliber (like a .308) will reach far enough to hit

the vitals and do enough damage on the way to kill the deer. Again, in doing so, it is almost assured to ruin a lot of one or both hind quarters, as well as making a mess internally. With all that said, if the large femoral artery that runs down both legs is pierced completely, the deer will die within seconds.

I could understand a hunter taking this shot at a trophy-class buck. But should a hunter take this desperate shot, the meat, as mangled as it might be, will only be good to use as ground and/or stew meat. What I have found about this position is if the deer is standing or slowly walking away from you, there is a very high percentage that it will eventually turn broadside before it goes too far—offering a

Photo credit: Ted Rose.

This could be the most terrible of all shots when it comes to destroying a majority of the deer meat. While it will kill the deer 99.9999 percent of the time, I would not suggest that hunters take this shot.

nice broadside shot. Novice hunters should definitely pass on taking a shot in this position.

Three of the five positions offer excellent standing shot placement opportunities, and the same **three** positions provide very good chances of shot placement at slowly walking deer. They do not all provide even semi-good shot placement opportunities at deer or other game that are walking fast, trotting, running, or moving flat out at warp speeds (finally, I got my *Star Trek* reference in).

Trying to shoot deer in any of the five positions mentioned above when they are walking, trotting, and/or running greatly lessens the chance of an instant kill. Worse off, there is a greater probability of hitting an area that is inevitably fatal but permits the deer to run long distances before dying. These areas include heart, lung (particularly when shot in only one lung), liver, kidneys, stomach, or intestines. Deer that are shot in these areas can run to a neighbor's land or state lands where other hunters have an opportunity to kill the deer. Again, these types of shots greatly reduce the chances of having prime tasting venison because of the significant increase in stress levels.

Deadly Shots

Shoulder Shot—The Deadliest of All Shot Placements

As I mentioned in the section above, this position is my absolute favorite. It is without question the best possible position to shoot an animal. When I see a deer or other big-game animal in a standing broadside position, my excitement and heart rate fall significantly. Why you ask? Because, with a shoulder shot, I know that my chances of killing the animal quickly, if not instantaneously, have just increased exponentially. If you want to increase your chances of killing your game quickly and/or instantly, while imparting an absolute minimum amount of stress, if any at all, then shooting at the shoulder blade on a standing animal will achieve those goals.

When it comes to accurate shot placement, the bones that a hunter can consider shooting are: the middle of the rib cage, cervical vertebrae, the spinal column, the lumbar and thoracic vertebrae, and the large scapula. The scapula, cervical vertebrae, and rib cage protect vital organs, veins and arteries, or a combination of them. The two skeletal areas on the list are the cervical vertebrae (neck bones) and the scapula. The neck shot offers a smaller target and if the bullet misses the cervical vertebrae it could lead to a

This buck presents the perfect position for a hunter to make a quick clean kill. A shot placed through the front shoulder will kill the deer before it hits the ground. Categorically there is no better shot than to hit the scapula; the deer will fall where it stood.

wounded and/or unrecovered deer. The shoulder blade (scapula) is a much larger target and therefore offers a higher rate of success.

Consequently, without question, shooting the scapula (shoulder blade) on any big game animal is always my first choice. Ninety-nine percent of the time, a shoulder shot will kill a deer almost instantly. It is not a target for small caliber deer rifles, however, as the bullet must penetrate through the heavy scapula bone to be deadly. Most often, the bullet will pass through the shoulder blade and break the spine, causing instant unconsciousness and paralysis. On its path it can also sever the arteries of dorsal aorta, aortic arch, the exterior and interior pectoral, and the posterior vena cava vein. If the bullet rattles around enough it can also pierce the top of the heart. Over my five-plus decades of shooting big game, I have found shooting the shoulder blade to be an absolutely deadly shot.

I only take this shot when deer or other big game are standing in place or walking *very* slowly. That's because the faster a deer moves, the more the shoulder blade moves back and forth, making it more difficult to shoot at the center of the shoulder blade, which is the area that does the most damage (particularly true for bowhunters). I recommend every deer hunter practice this shot by using full-size cardboard and/or other types of deer targets. This one-shot placement zone can increase your instant kill ratio tenfold, and your overall kill ratio. It also provides top-quality tasting venison.

Brain Shot

A shot to the deer's brain will kill the deer instantly. And, yes, like the shoulder shot, it will reduce or completely eliminate any stress to the animal, due to the quickness in dispatching the deer. In turn, this will improve the overall quality, flavor, tenderness, and maximum cooking potential of the meat. However, for a few reasons, a brain shot might not be the best choice. It is certainly not a shot if you intend to mount the buck's antlers. Another caution here is that hitting the brain isn't all that easy, as it is a very small target. If it is missed, more than likely the shot will cause significant trauma to the face of the deer. A potentially missed brain shot is something to avoid at all costs, as the deer will run

Photo credit: Ted Rose.

Let's face it, a deer shot in the brain will be dead before it hits the ground. However, this is a shot that should only be taken at close range. For the DIY butcher, this shot will maximize the amount of undamaged deer meat.

off and suffer a long and dreadful death. An errant brain shot can also lead to missing the deer completely.

On the other hand, if the most important element of the hunt is preserving as much edible meat as possible with as little gun-shot damage to other meat, then a brain shot should be considered with caveats. First and foremost, brain shots should only be taken at standing deer. That bears repeating: at standing deer. The closer they are to you, the better off you'll be, as short distances increase success ratios for brain shots. Over the last fifty-plus years of hunting, the few times I shot game in the brain were when the deer was standing within a distance of twenty yards or less. I recommend this shot only to those whose shooting skills are superb. Brain-shot deer are dead before they hit the ground, and, therefore, there is no question that the best quality of meat will be obtained using this shot.

Heart Shot

Hunters are often surprised to hear that I avoid taking heart shots. The reason is that heart shots can be problematic, especially when the deer is moving slowly. A standing deer that is shot in the heart has a significant chance to run off before dying. Sometimes they can cover one hundred or more yards before they collapse dead. This results in the animal being stressed as it pumps excess adrenaline chemicals through its system before expiring.

It is also a small target and one that is easily missed—sometimes even by a couple of inches. The portion of the heart located below the lungs is a very small (but lethal) area about five to seven inches in profile on an average adult deer, and three to five inches on smaller deer. It should be noted here that although a heart-shot deer can still be pumping some blood for a short time, if the bullet severs the large blood vessels (arteries and veins)

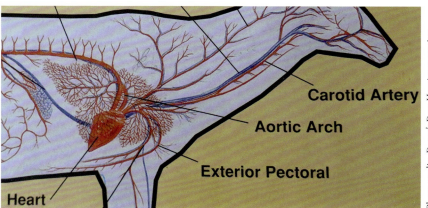

Photo credit: *Deer & Deer Hunting* magazine.

I am not a big fan of shooting the heart, as a heart-shot deer can run one hundred yards or more. This is not a shot to take if there is a concern that the deer can run onto private property.

that connect to the top of the heart, the deer's blood pressure will drop to zero and it will die somewhat instantly.

Lung Shot

Shooting at the lungs tops the list as one of the most shot-at organs of deer and other big game. To be frank, they should be. They offer the largest target of vitals, particularly when the deer is standing or walking *slowly* while broadside to the hunter. A hunter doesn't have to be a crack-shot to hit the lungs either. Because of the large size of the overall area they cover, the lungs also offer a good target at long distances. Deer shot in the lungs usually run hard, fast, and straight at first. But they quickly slow down as they find it hard to breathe, and soon thereafter collapse. Generally, they rarely go farther than one hundred yards after a bullet or broadhead has penetrated *both* lungs.

Many times, I have seen double-lung-shot deer run off fast and die in fewer than fifty yards. As a majority of hunters know, the lungs are a good choice as an area to consider for shot placement. The downside to

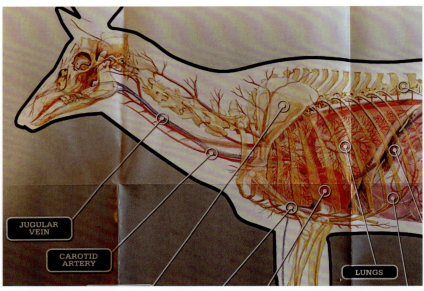

JUGULAR VEIN

CAROTID ARTERY

LUNGS

Photo credit: *Deer & Deer Hunting magazine.*

Traditionally, the lungs are a very dependable shot to shoot a deer. The lungs present the largest kill zone; thus it is hard to miss what is being aimed at. The downsides are a larger loss of meat, plus the deer can run one hundred or more yards before dying.

shooting at the lungs is if the bullet caliber is too small (or broadhead too light) and if it gets deflected before hitting the deer, it is possible only one lung will be penetrated. Most times, this ends in a lost deer. Even when shooting at the lungs with a larger caliber, there is always the possibility of the projectile hitting a branch or other object that causes the bullet to only pierce one lung. In the end, deer shot in one lung rarely die instantly. This causes adrenaline to pump through the deer's body, reducing the overall meat quality. Again, unfortunately, we're dealing with a running, stressed animal that doesn't die instantly. I know this is repetitive, but a principal message within this book. It's vital to make a good killing shot that results in a quick, or better yet, instant death, to ensure quality meat. That's something to think about (before the shot) if you want to maximize the taste of your venison.

Liver Shot

The liver is located in the middle of the deer's chest cavity and is directly behind the diaphragm, just behind the lungs. In my opinion, it is a highly risky place to aim for, even though the liver is the largest organ in a deer. If the bullet is off in any direction behind it (toward the rear of the deer), the bullet could hit the rumen or the large or small intestines. Neither area is a good option and usually ends up with an unrecovered deer. Most often a deer hit in the liver will lunge forward and then quickly run off. Moreover, a deer shot in the liver takes time to die.

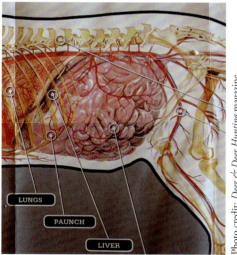

LUNGS

PAUNCH

LIVER

Photo credit: Deer & Deer Hunting magazine.

The liver is usually hit by accident. It is not a prime target and should not be considered as such. Moreover, a liver shot takes time to kill the deer. The meat ends up compromised from stress and the chemicals released by adrenaline.

Obviously, this is not a good scenario when it comes to preserving the flavor of the meat. Sometimes, it may take the animal several hours to succumb to the wound. But the end result will be a dead deer. Most liver shots happen by accident, and I think that's better than purposefully aiming for the liver.

Kidney Shot

This scenario is almost identical to the liver shot. Like the liver, the kidney is not an organ that should be targeted. Most deer hit in the kidneys were shot there accidently. Other than not taking this shot intentionally, there isn't much more to be said about it.

Carotid Artery Shot

The carotid artery is in the lower part of the neck leading toward the lungs. When the carotid artery is *completely* severed, the deer can succumb to the injury within seconds. It is important to note that I am not talking about injuries to smaller arteries or veins that will also lead to the demise of the deer. I am referring to a major artery that was severed. A deer must lose about 30 percent of its blood before it dies. So, you can see how drastic severing the carotid artery actually is when it causes the deer to die within seconds from being severed. While most wounds result in shock, an arterial wound, like that of the carotid artery, causes shock to occur quickly due to the speed of how fast the blood bleeds out of the deer. With all that said, however, this is not a shot I would recommend. It isn't a consistent high-success target, as the area being aimed at has a very narrow point of impact. If the projectile misses the carotid artery and the other vitals within the deer's neck, and it only passes through muscle, the odds of recovering

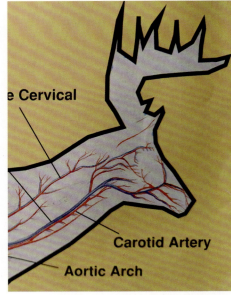

Photo credit: *Deer & Deer Hunting magazine.*

The carotid artery is a devastating kill shot. When it is completely severed, the deer will die in seconds. It is a small target, though, and therefore it is not one to take without detailed knowledge of its exact location within the deer's neck.

the deer are small. If the carotid artery is severed completely, though, the reaction of the deer will be as if you took a sledgehammer and struck the deer extremely hard in the back of the head.

Circulatory System

The circulatory system contains all the major and minor arteries and veins. Other than the heart and the jugular vein, most hunters don't purposefully aim for the veins and arteries in a deer, and wisely so. When selecting a particular organ, bone, or skeletal area for your shot placement, however, you should be very familiar with what arteries and veins are found near or attached to them. The fact is the major arteries including the femoral artery, dorsal aorta, aortic arch, carotid artery, and the exterior and interior pectoral arteries are all close by, attached, lying directly under, behind, or covering major organs and bones. Being familiar with their locations is not enough. To be effective with your shot placement choices, knowing *exactly* where the large arteries and veins are within circulatory systems will give you a tremendous edge in making one-shot kills.

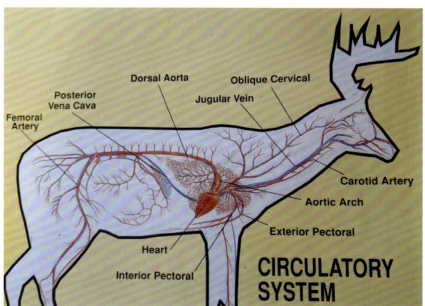

Photo credit: *Deer & Deer Hunting* magazine.

In order to kill a deer quickly and humanely, it is important to learn all you can about the deer's circulatory system. Visit www.shopdeerhunting.com/deer-and-deer-hunting-shot-placement-poster to buy an enlightening poster on this subject.

Many hunters have had deer step out in front of them only to automatically place the crosshairs on the animal's rib cage in order to shoot it through the lungs. While that shot will prove to be fatal a majority of the time, it is not a shot for those who want to preserve the meat. Hopefully, this section has helped you to understand more about whitetail anatomy and its relationship to excellent shot placement, which results in significantly reducing stress to the animals you're hunting and enhancing all the elements of better tasting venison.

Adrenaline and Stress

Up to this point, I've repeatedly talked about eliminating stress to an animal. For that reason, the following information is necessary in order to provide you with a more in-depth idea of what stress actually does to a deer. The long and the short of it is that "the stress factor" causes any meat (wild or domestic) to taste less than flavorful. The greater the stress factor, the lesser the quality of meat. Rather than bore you with a lot of scientific mumbo jumbo, I'll cut to the chase and give you a short scientific version of what stress does to deer meat.

Most muscles in humans and other mammals work similarly to each other. Each contraction of a muscle works by passing one protein, actin, past another protein, myosin, to shorten the muscles. The energy for muscle contraction derives from chemical reactions in all animals. These chemical responses require energy (fuel) gained from whatever the deer has eaten over the preceding twelve hours (which breaks down into blood sugar [glucose]). All muscle reaction requires that the muscles be kept warm to operate at their peak. In a deer, this is achieved by the amount of fat under its skin, blood flow, and the deer's thick coat, all providing the critical elements necessary to create the chemical reactions that produce energy.

All of these elements allow the muscles in a deer to chemically produce a vital product called adenosine triphosphate (ATP). ATP is the chemical that initiates two key muscle proteins to slip past each other. It splits into smaller sub-chemicals (which are recycled repeatedly) and releases fuel that causes muscle contraction. The result of ATP allows a deer's muscles to contract for it to walk, run, jump, eat, mate, and perform all other activities. There is a crucial job that ATP performs: It allows two muscle contraction proteins (actin and myosin) to separate, allowing the muscle to relax. Basically, ATP allows the muscles to contract and, equally important, relax. A muscle that can't relax becomes stiff and remains in the last position it was in when the ATP is no longer produced. This is what happens when rigor mortis sets in.

In all meat that we eat (domestic or wild), there are enzymes and minerals that leak into the muscles when the animal dies. These enzymes and minerals break down the proteins in the muscles and the connective tissues around and in the muscles. The enzymes cause the muscles to relax after rigor mortis. An ideal amount of time needed to allow these enzymes and minerals to work their magic is one to two days.

In a healthy and relaxed deer, the glycogen content of its muscles is high. After it is shot and dies quickly, the glycogen in the muscles is converted into lactic acid, and the muscle and carcass set into rigor mortis. This lactic acid is necessary to produce meat, which is tasteful and tender. If the animal is stressed before it is killed, the glycogen is used up, and the lactic acid level that develops in the meat after it is dead is significantly reduced. This will have serious adverse effects on meat quality. So, as I mentioned in the beginning of this chapter, killing a deer as quickly as possible and without stressing it prior to being killed (alerting the deer to your presence, pushing it on a deer drive, or crippling or wounding it) is crucial to more appealing meat.

I know I said I wouldn't bore you with a lot of scientific information, but trust me, this is the short version of why hunters should avoid stressing a deer he/she is about to kill. Again, a stressed animal will have greater muscle contraction (and an accompanying increase in adrenaline) and that will subsequently affect the flavor of the meat. This is why one-shot kills to deer and other big game that are unaware of the hunter's presence are so important to better tasting venison.

My wife, Kate, is the director of operations of New York Custom Processing, LLC (NYCP), a custom beef butchering plant owned by long-time, renowned meat processing guru Joseph (Joe) Rocco and dairy and cattle ranchers, Bob and Jack Curtin. NYCP is overseen daily by an onsite United States Department of Agriculture (USDA) food safety inspector as well as a doctor of veterinarian medicine. NYCP is also routinely inspected and certified as an animal welfare-approved facility to make sure all the animals being processed at the plant are treated humanely prior to being killed. Reducing, if not eliminating stress to the animals is one of NYCP's highest priorities. At NYCP, the cattle producers and, equally important, NYCP's high-profile clients are all dedicated to making sure the animals don't undergo any unnecessary stress from the moment the animals are unloaded until the moment they are dispatched.

This practice has two primary elements. The first is the humane treatment of the animals processed at the plant and the second point, equally important to all involved, is to ensure that each carcass provides the best possible product to the end users—restaurant purveyors, restaurants, schools, supermarkets, and homes.

I mention this for two reasons: First, to drive home the point that prime tasting beef, pork, veal, and lamb doesn't occur by luck at quality processing plants. For instance, NYCP puts a lot of detailed planning and adheres stringently to every USDA regulation in order to reduce stress and other negative factors to the meat processed at the plant.

The second point is that hunters who desire exceptional tasting meat from their deer are obliged to put as much forethought into

Photo credit: Fiduccia Enterprises.

This is New York Custom Processing, LLC's plant. Beef processed in this USDA plant is for both national clients and local customers.

taking and butchering their deer as if they were butchering a beef. This includes dispatching the deer as quickly as possible, quickly and properly field dressing it, draining the body cavity and wiping out as much blood as possible, quickly ventilating the body cavity, removing the deer from the woods, thoroughly cleaning (rinsing out) the body cavity, and cooling the deer (again) as quickly as possible. Quickly lowering the temperature of the carcass is one of the most critical elements to good tasting venison. Attention is also necessary regarding removing the hide (as soon as is possible and practical), quartering the carcass, butchering it properly in a clean environment, and properly packaging and freezing it. By paying attention to these factors, hunters will increase the flavor, tenderness, and overall edibility of their meat ten-fold.

Shot Placement Tips

1. The number one cause of poor shot placement is uncontrollable excitement, a.k.a. buck fever. Buck fever is a phenomenon caused by a surge of adrenaline, but it can be a curable ailment.

2. Shooting at a running or trotting deer is another major cause of hunters missing their shot or wounding a deer.

3. Accurate shot placement occurs when using a solid rest, including a sturdy branch, backpack, tripod shooting sticks, and/or a shooting bag to rest on a rail of a tree stand or an open hunting blind.

4. Some game is missed or wounded when hunters do not look carefully at what is between the end of the barrel and the deer. Bullets can be deflected and dramatically sent off course by even a thin branch.

5. The cleaner the firearm's barrel, the more accurate the shot.

6. When aiming at a deer that flags its tail sideways twice, the hunter usually has fewer than fifteen seconds to shoot before the deer moves off.

7. To increase your chances of making an accurate shot, don't look at the antlers too long. Instead, concentrate on the exact spot (for instance, the shoulder blade) you want to shoot.

8. Wipe your scope lens clean regularly during your hunt. This prevents the lens from fogging up and provides a crystal-clear sight window should a deer show up.

9. Using proper breathing techniques is an important element to better shooting accuracy.

10. Dry firing (modern firearms) is a highly effective practice that will enhance shooting skills. Make sure the firearm is unloaded before dry firing it. I'll repeat that, double check that your firearm is empty prior to practicing aiming and pulling the trigger.

11. Increase your kill ratio success by eliminating risky shots.

12. A high-quality riflescope results in a much better sight window, which in turn allows for more accurate shot placement.

Bowhunting Recovery Times

An important factor to recovering bowhunted deer is keeping calm before and after the shot. After the shot, there are several important questions bowhunters must ask themselves to successfully find their deer, including:

- Where was the deer standing when it was hit?
- Where did the broadhead impact the body?
- How did the deer react immediately after the shot?
- Was it a good hit or a bad hit?

Once you know the answers to these points, you'll be able to make the correct decisions about how long to wait before looking for the deer.

IMPACT AREA	TIME TO WAIT BEFORE TRAILING
Lungs	20 to 30 minutes
Heart	20 minutes
Liver	2 to 3 hours
Paunch	4 to 24 hours

IMPACT AREA	TIME TO WAIT BEFORE TRAILING
Intestines	6 to 24 hours
Muscle	20 to 30 minutes
Spine	Follow up ASAP

Sources: *Deer and Deer Hunting Magazine*, Archery Trade Association, Bowhunters Association.

Chapter 3

Field Dressing Deer

———

Once a deer has expired, the goal from that point on is to make sure it is field dressed carefully and properly. The fact is, a hunter can do plenty of harm to the palatability and overall quality of the meat during the field dressing process. This usually happens when a hunter unintentionally punctures the colon, bladder, stomach, or intestines.

The mistakes made immediately after eviscerating the deer usually include not removing as much blood as possible from the body cavity after the innards are removed and not cooling the carcass immediately thereafter. After that, it is important not to get mud and other forest debris in the body cavity as the deer is being dragged out. Yet another mistake is not covering the carcass in a quality game bag as soon as it is hung on the game pole. You can trust that all of these factors will *negatively* affect the tenderness, flavor, and cookability of your prized wild game meat. Therefore, it is important to field dress a deer properly in order to have prime tasting venison.

Field Dressing Mythologies

There are as many myths about how to field dress a deer, as there are folk-lores and half-truths about most subjects about deer hunting (information about the rut, scrapes, rubs, moon phase theories, and so on). For example, as a young hunter I was taught that it was absolutely necessary to remove the tarsal glands before field dressing a deer, as the tarsal glands could taint the meat and/or make the meat taste gamey. As I gained more field-dressing experience, however, it didn't take me long to discover that the information about removing the tarsal glands was simply not true. As long as you don't touch the tarsal glands with your hands or knife blade, there is little to no chance at all that the tarsal glands will make the meat taste gamey or taint it. They simply have to be left alone.

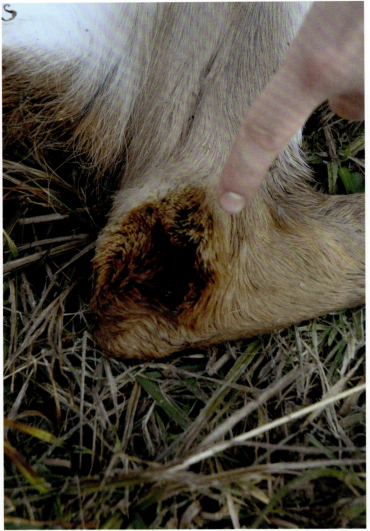

Photo credit: Fiduccia Enterprises.

The misnomer that the tarsal gland spoils the meat is nothing more than an old wives' tale.

Bleeding Out

Another ill-advised recommendation about field dressing is to slit the deer's throat in order to properly bleed it out. As any hunter who has field dressed a deer can testify, once the deer is shot, most of the blood quickly drains into the body cavity. Cutting the deer's neck to bleed it out is simply not necessary. This is particularly true if you are going to mount the buck's antlers. Slitting the throat will ruin the hide for the taxidermist if he is going to make a full shoulder mount.

Opening the Entire Body Cavity

Another piece of misinformation about eviscerating a deer is to cut open the entire body cavity from the bottom of the lowest point of the abdomen (between the hams) to the very top of the deer's neck below its white throat patch. While this might hasten the field-dressing process, it can create problems. Firstly, this technique of field dressing often increases the chance that a hunter will unintentionally puncture the bladder, colon, and/or intestines. That ends up spilling urine and feces into the cavity. Equally worrisome, it is possible that you could unintentionally cut into some of the prime meat on the hind quarters. Secondly, if you're field dressing a buck and intend to get a full shoulder mount, this is definitely not the way to field dress a deer. Consequently, hunters should disregard the above-mentioned myths and abide by the facts regarding how to properly field dress a deer.

The Correct Way to Field Dress a Deer

It is essential for hunters, especially novices, to learn how to effectively field dress deer in a way that is most comfortable for them. While most other hunting skills and tactics can be done in a more relaxed manner, when it comes to field dressing deer, it must be done as quickly as possible to allow the body heat to rapidly dissipate to help preserve the overall quality of the meat. With that said, though, keep in mind that razor-sharp tools are being used. Field dressing, therefore, must be done while keeping safety uppermost in mind.

Before field dressing a deer, take a moment to realize its meat will provide you with tender cuts of flavorful steaks, loins, roasts, burger, ribs, stew, sausage, and jerky meat. To safeguard your prized bounty, you must

Photo credit: Fiduccia Enterprises.

Soon after celebrating taking a buck, it is important to begin field dressing it. Kate took this buck in 2017 on our farm. Within an hour after taking this photo, the buck was field dressed, skinned, and hung to cool.

eviscerate and cool the body cavity with utmost care. Care should also be taken when dragging the deer out, cooling it further on the game pole, removing the hide, and covering the body cavity with a quality game bag as soon as practical. All these things will influence the flavor and quality of deer meat.

When it comes to the process of field dressing a deer, the fact is that there are only a couple of correct ways to do it. The following tips and instructions include the most common way to field dress deer. The order of the field-dressing process can vary from hunter to hunter, however.

Field Dressing Step #1. Due to the possibility of contacting Lyme disease, first put on field-dressing gloves before beginning to field dress the deer. Place the deer on as flat a surface as is practical and then turn it over on its back (or side). The head should be slightly higher than the rest of the body cavity, so gravity will help the entrails slide out more easily when they are cut free.

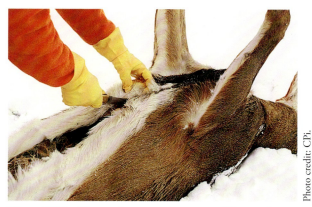

To avoid blood-borne diseases, protect yourself by covering your hands and arms with field dressing gloves. Shoulder-high gloves will offer the most protection from ticks and such.

Photo credit: CPi.

Field Dressing Step #2. The best way to remove the colon and bladder is by using a clever device called a Butt Out 2 tool made by Hunters Special-ties. Slowly insert the pointed end of the tool all the way into the deer's anal cavity. Push it inward until the round plastic portion of the tool (directly below the handle) presses flat against the anus. Twist the tool a time or two or until you feel it grab onto the inner intestinal anal membrane. This typically takes several turns. Then slowly and steadily pull the tool out. It will remove about a ten- to twelve-inch section of the intestinal tract to the outside of the body cavity. Almost the entire section will be filled with pel-lets or dung. When the pellets end, the anal tract will look white and free of pellets. Once it is clear, an option is to tightly tie off the intestine with a string to prevent any remaining fluids from leaking back into the body cav-ity. Lastly, cut the membrane at its clearest point to free the tool. Once the anal tract is removed, the rest of the field-dressing process will be accom-plished more quickly and effectively. For more information about the Butt Out 2 tool, visit www.hunterspec.com/product/butt-out-2.

Photo credit: Hunters Specialties.

A Butt Out tool makes short work of removing the anal tract. More important, it prevents spilling deer pellets and fluids into the carcass.

Field Dressing Step #3. Make a shallow two-to three-inch-long cut on the side of the penis or, on a doe, the udder. Separate the external reproductive organs of a buck from the abdominal wall. On a doe, remove the udder. Be careful doing this as milk sours quickly in the udder. Sour milk has a foul smell that can give the meat a disagreeable taste. Before removing the genitals, check with local game regulations. Some states require that the

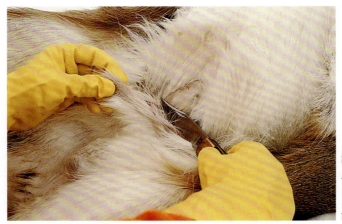

Photo credit: CPi

Before removing the sex organs of deer, check the local game laws to make sure it is legal to do so.

genitals remain attached to the carcass, in the event the deer is brought to a required check station. If it is legal, carefully cut them free and let them hang over the back of the anus. It is important not to cut them free of the viscera at this point.

Field Dressing Step #4. With the deer on its back, straddle it so you are facing its head. Pinch a piece of skin in the belly section and pull it up and away from the body. Insert the tip of the knife blade and make a shallow slit into the muscle of the skin, which will prevent accidently puncturing the intestines. Make the cut just long enough to insert two fingers. Form a V with your fingers and carefully continue to slit a thin layer of abdomen muscle and skin all the way up to the sternum. As you make this cut, the intestines and stomach will begin to push out of the body cavity but will not fall free as they are still attached by connective tissue.

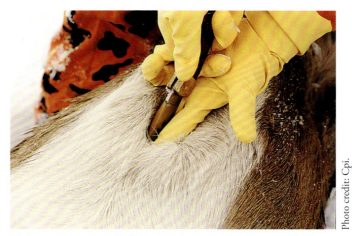

Photo credit: Cpi.

Make sure this cut is shallow enough to avoid puncturing the intestines.

Field Dressing Step #5. If you are not going to mount the deer's head, the next step is to make a cut through the rib cage. While straddling the deer, slightly bend your knees and face the head. With the knife blade facing up, position the knife under the breastbone. Hold the knife with both hands for leverage and cut through the cartilage in the center of breastbone. Continue cutting up through the neck. If you intend to mount the deer's head, stop at the brisket line and skip Step #6.

Photo credit: Cpi.

If you intend to get a full shoulder mount of your deer, don't cut this high. Instead, stop cutting just below the brisket.

Field Dressing Step #6. Once the neck is open, free the windpipe and esophagus by cutting the connective tissue. Grasp them firmly and pull them down toward the body cavity while continuing to cut any connective tissues as you proceed.

Field Dressing Step #7. If you are going to mount the deer's head, you will have to tie off the gullet, or throat. Push it forward as far as possible, and cut if free from the windpipe. Also cut around the diaphragm and remove the connective tissue of the lungs and other organs. Now carefully reach up as far as you can—as far as your arms will allow—into the throat area to sever the esophagus and trachea. Be careful of your knife blade, as most accidents occur during this step when you can't see what you're cutting. Cuts made to fingers can be severe and they can cause profuse bleeding.

Field Dressing Step #8. If you haven't removed the rectum using a Butt Out 2 tool, you will have to address the job the traditional way at this point. Some prefer to remove the rectal tract and urethra by slicing between the hams or splitting the pelvic bone. Others remove the anal tract first by placing the point of a knife to the side of the rectum and making a cut that completely encircles the rectum. Free the rectum and urethra by loosening the connective tissue with the tip of the blade. To prevent any leakage from the anal tract or the urethra, tie it off with a heavy piece of string. The next step is the trickiest part of whole process. Push the tied-off rectum and urethra under the pelvic bone and into the body cavity. If you choose to, you may opt to split the pelvic bone, which makes removing the rectum and urethra easier, but it requires using a stout knife or small axe.

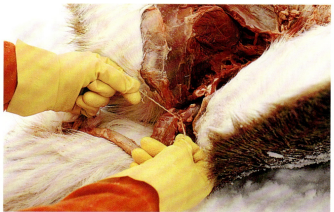

This is the traditional way of removing the colon. Make sure you tie the string's knot tightly to avoid spillage of deer feces.

Field Dressing Step #9. Grasp one side of the rib cage firmly with one hand and pull it open. Cut all the remaining connective tissue along the

Removing the gullet and pulling it free is where most accidents take place when field dressing.

diaphragm free from the rib opening down to the backbone. While cutting, stay as close to the rib cage as possible. Be careful not to puncture the stomach, intestines, or any other internal matter. Next, repeat the same thing on the other side so both cuts meet over the backbone.

Now reach up and grasp the windpipe and esophagus and pull them down and away from the body cavity. Detach the heart and liver. Now all the innards should be free of any connective tissue, allowing you to scoop out any remaining entrails onto the ground along with as much blood as possible from the body cavity.

Field Dressing Step #10. Once all the entrails have been eviscerated from the deer's body cavity, it is crucial to dissipate the heat from the cavity as rapidly as possible. Prop the body cavity open with a stick or, better yet, a lightweight locking stainless-steel rib-cage spreader made by Outdoor Edge (www.outdooredge.com).

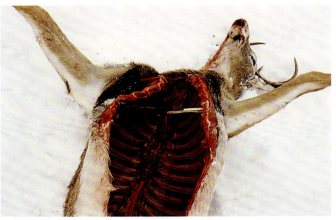

Photo credit: CPi.

If you don't have a stainless-steel rib-sage spreader, a sturdy stick will do. A folding rib-cage spreader comes in a small carry-case that will conveniently fit in a backpack.

If at all possible when you are in the field, wash out the body cavity with water or snow. Remove as much dirt, debris, excess blood, and so on as possible. Wash the body cavity out more thoroughly again when the deer is brought back to camp or home. Hanging the deer on the game pole as soon as possible will go a long way to enhance the cooling process. If hanging the deer isn't possible, turn it over with the open body cavity down and let any remaining blood or fluids drain away.

Finally, an important element when field dressing, skinning, and ultimately butchering deer and other game animals is to protect yourself from a variety of health issues (ticks, CWD, blood-borne diseases) and safety issues (splintered bones, a slip of a knife, etc.). Always use a pair of quality field-dressing gloves. If you are like me and are allergic to latex, buy gloves made of Nitrile or some other material instead. Gloves made of Nitrile are 100 percent latex-free and powder-free, plus they are ambidextrous.

My best advice about field-dressing gloves is to avoid buying cheaply made ones that usually cost a dollar or two. They can easily tear during use and offer less protection than more expensive field-dressing gloves. Shoulder-length field-dressing gloves are better than gloves that just cover your hands. Hunters Specialties and/or HME gloves and a host of other companies make shoulder-length gloves that generally sell for about six to eight dollars a packet.

The most effective heavy-duty latex-free field-dressing gloves for deer (and other game and fish) are made by Nitro Products (a world-renowned glove manufacturer) and are called ButcherSkinz. These black nitrile heavy-duty game-processing cloves have the perfect combination of dura-bility and grip. ButcherSkinz are also puncture resistant and won't rip as easily as latex or vinyl sometimes does. They also have a form-fitting design in order to get the job done more efficiently. ButcherSkinz are available at all the big box stores (Bass Pro Shops, Cabela's, Dicks, etc.,) as well as on Amazon and eBay. They cost ten to fifteen dollars, but are absolutely worth the price.

Keep It Insect-Free

A high priority when dressing a deer is to keep the carcass as free of insects as is possible. No one wants to eat meat that cheese flies, houseflies, mos-quitoes, and dreaded blowflies have laid their eggs on. These and a host of other insects, if given the slightest chance, will deposit their maggots in your deer meat with no sense of regret. I address this in more detail in a later chapter.

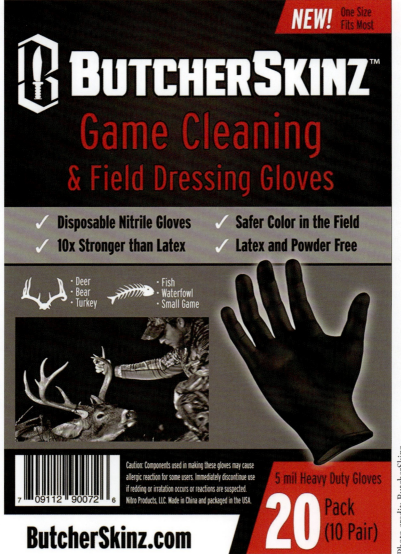

Chapter 4

From Field to Meat Pole

During the first several years I hunted deer, I never gave much thought to how I was going to get my deer out of the woods. I paid little attention to what was on the ground that I dragged my deer over, under, or through. I never gave any thought to dragging the body cavity over mud, through stagnant water, over decaying leaves, or over other forest debris. At the time, I was a solid one hundred eighty pounds and dragging a deer from the field back to my vehicle posed little problem for me. Once I reached my vehicle, hoisting the deer onto the roof and roping it securely in place was also done without much thought or physical effort. Worse yet, I paid no mind to how I would keep the carcass free of road dirt, fumes, insects, and other contaminants

Tying a deer to the hood or trunk of a vehicle was common from the 1960s to the mid-1990s. In New York, seeing deer tied to vehicles, streaming down Route 17 or the New York State Thruway was part and parcel of deer season. These sights spurred unbridled anticipation for countless hunters who hadn't filled their deer tags yet.

as I drove home. In those days, however, there was no choice about putting the deer on the hood, roof, or in the trunk of the vehicle, as it was illegal in New York to transport a dead deer and not have it visible on the outside of the vehicle.

I suspect most hunters of that era (circa 1960s), whether they lived in New York or not, gave little consideration to placing a deer on a vehicle and driving long and/or even short distances with it exposed to the weather and road grime. It was common to see countless deer displayed proudly on vehicles as hunters drove home with their game. It took me a couple of years to realize I should cover the deer with a game bag when transporting it home.

Lesson Learned

It wasn't until I moved to Crawford, Colorado in 1972 that the importance of preserving the tenderness and flavor of deer meat was made to me. It was during my first hunt with a friend of mine named Jim. We were hunting mule deer in the backcountry, on an elongated plateau at the top of Saddle Mountain. As we stalked along the edge of the ridge, I was watching a myriad of game trails that were made by deer, elk,

Photo credit: mountainproject.com

Centered in the picture is the majestic Needle Rock. To the right and behind it are the snow-capped peaks called Saddle Mountain, where Jim and I hunted. In the lower left-hand corner, nestled in pinions, is my old house.

and bear that regularly traversed the mountainside. We were slowly poking along the edge of the mesa toward its most southern point when I noticed a buck meandering along one of the game trails below. The buck was only about one hundred yards away when I first spied him. I was about to shoot at the buck when Jim whispered, "Let him pass, Needle Rock."

My friends and neighbors called me "Needle Rock Pete" because our house and forty acres bordered a famous monument called "Needle Rock." My cowboy buddies were original thinkers, huh? My former house and Needle Rock are located just a few miles from the hamlet of Crawford in Delta County, Colorado. Needle Rock is a remnant of volcanic plug that pushed up through the earth's crust about twenty-eight million years ago. It stands about one thousand feet tall above the floor of the Smith Fork of the Gunnison River within the western edge of the West Elk Mountains in western central Colorado (where I spent countless hours fishing for trout). It is an impressive sight, and can be seen from miles around that area. My house and land were eventually sold to the singer Joe Cocker. But I am getting sidetracked here, so let me get back to my story.

Jim was a well-known hunter with decades of experience. When he suggested I let the buck pass, I lowered my Winchester .270 without any hesitation, and watched as the buck disappeared into the black timber. After the buck was out of sight, I asked him about his remark. As usual, his response was to the point, but noteworthy. "The trail he was on is steep and filled with slide rock and deadfalls. It would have taken the rest of the day to drag him out, and we were sure to skin up the hide and beat up the meat," he said matter-of-factly. I should mention that all my quotes of Jim from here on are recalled as closely as my memory can recollect.

Jim made his living as a cattle rancher. He had a distinctive look that thoroughly portrayed his six decades of wisdom. His well-seasoned face had wrinkles that appeared almost to be leathery, but it also had a striking masculine cowboy look to it. Jim was never one for being long on words, but he was equally never short on passing along sage advice either.

Sometime later we saw a young buck as it walked through a stand of quaking aspen. Jim was also never one to be concerned about the size of a buck's antlers. Instead, his main objective was to take an immature buck. As he was fond of saying, "they eat well" (at the time, no one shot does in Colorado). The buck stopped every few feet to browse on fallen aspen leaves. Jim patiently waited until the slow walking buck stopped. When it

Photo credit: Fiduccia Enterprises.

Circa 1975, here I am holding the antlers of the mule deer buck Jim shot. Jim was never about antler size; he was always about the meat. Beside me is my dog Daisy.

did, he dropped it in its tracks with one clean shot through the shoulder (another well-learned lesson for me).

While field dressing the buck, Jim talked about how he felt it was critical to take care of game meat. The conversation lasted longer than he had ever talked to me during the years I knew him. He began by saying "Ya know, Needle Rock, I take care of my deer meat better than I do my dawg, and I love that damn dawg." For the record, so-help-me, Jim's dog's name was "Dawg." From there, he covered more points than I can recall here.

After the entrails were removed, Jim dragged the buck several yards away. With the deer lying on its underside, he splayed the buck's front and back legs wide apart. Then he asked me to lift the rear legs as he lifted the two front ones. We held them up and vigorously shook the deer back and forth and up and down, draining almost all the blood out of the body cavity. Then we placed it down in a blood-free area a few feet away. I watched, with a look of curiosity, as Jim, obviously not satisfied with how much blood was drained out, took out a few clean rags from his backpack and wiped away the remaining blood. He saw the questioning look on my face and looked directly in my eyes and said, as best as I can remember, "If my game meat is to taste as good as my cattle meat, Needle Rock, then I have to treat it the same way I treat the beef I slaughter." To this day, I'll never forget all the things Jim said to me on Saddle Mountain, particularly about wanting his game meat to taste as good as his cattle beef. That single piece of advice was the genesis of me making sure all my venison would taste as delicious as a well taken care of piece of quality beef.

But my lesson didn't end there. As we dragged the buck to where we had tied the horses, I noticed Jim avoided taking the buck over as much forest debris as possible, including downed trees, rocks, and, particularly, areas strewn with gravel and cow dung. In the West, ranchers who have permits let their cattle run free on Bureau of Land Management (BLM). Naturally, there are a lot of old and fresh cow-pies in some of the best hunting country in the West. Dragging his deer's open body cavity over them was obviously what Jim was trying to avoid.

When we got back to the horses and mule, Jim reached into his saddle bag and removed a large, neatly folded tarp and spread it out on the ground. I asked him what he was doing, and he said, "I'm going to quarter up my buck, son, that's what I intend to do." I suggested we could just throw the buck on the back of the mule and pack him out. Again, Jim's reply was short, but right to the point. "Nope, ain't gonna do that, Needle Rock. It's a long dusty ride back down the mountain."

After quartering the buck, we took the pieces and slid them into separate game bags, then placed them into the panniers (large carrier bags made of heavy-duty canvas or leather placed over a wooden pack saddle). Panniers are slung over the back of a horse or a beast of burden—in this case, Ned, the mule.

Once they were in the panniers, Jim quietly said, "They'll stay cool and dirt-free on ride back down the mountain." Then he paused briefly, and with the best smile Jim could muster, he said, "Besides, Needle Rock, dangling a buck off old Ned here would only encourage him to bite and kick me more than he does."

I learned valuable lessons that day, even one to avoid over-packing a mule and/or getting bit or kicked by Ned. That wise old man made an impact on me that day. From then on, I treated deer and other big game I shot with more attention to their care. I made a point to field dress them properly, dissipate heat from the cavity, drain excess blood, and protect the meat so it got home as unsoiled as possible.

Extraction Options

Other than on hunting trips into wilderness backcountry areas, getting a deer out and back to deer camp or home is a lot different than it was in the sixties and seventies. I could fill pages of this chapter with a myriad of deer-extracting devices. Some include products and other methods used to take out whitetails, mule deer, and black bear. Larger game like moose, elk, caribou, bear, and so on as a rule are generally quartered and packed out by horses, mules, boats, Argos, or large RTV units by guides and/or hunters.

There are several ways to drag or extract deer and other big game from the field. Some are backbreaking, others are backbreaking and dangerous, a few are cumbersome but useful, and others make the chore short work. Below are some suggestions about the good, bad, and ugly extraction methods that can be used or totally avoided.

Unsafe Deer Extraction Systems

I am seventy-one years old and over the years have used a lot of tactics for removing deer from the woods. These experiences allow me to offer this sage advice: Avoid removing deer by using pole carrying methods. These removal methods are dangerous and require strength and manual labor. The manual pole carrying systems include two hunters carrying a deer out that is tethered to a single pole. The pole is then placed on each of the hunters' shoulders as they carry the deer out over uneven ground, downed logs, through creeks, so forth. This extraction process is painful and dangerous. If you are young, strong, and enjoy removing deer rustically, consider a cleverer way than using a single log pole. Instead, make a stretcher-type device made from two log poles and strap the deer in. Make sure the poles are capable of supporting the animal's weight. At least this system allows the hunters to each carry two poles, one in each hand. It also provides a system that lowers the deer's center of gravity. With that said, even this technique should only be used if absolutely necessary.

Another more practical variation to the stretcher device is to make a travois. Basically, it's nothing more than a stretcher-like device that is dragged by one or more people. In the movie *The Revenant*, Leonardo DiCaprio was critically mauled by a grizzly bear. The device his companions made to take him with them was a travois. It's fashioned out of sturdy tree limbs and stout cord. This is the safest pole carrying extraction device (of the two mentioned above). It allows the lower half of the deer's body, where most of its weight is, to be nearer the ground, making it easier for the hunters to drag the device. These methods also require that hunters carry equipment such as axes, ropes, and so on.

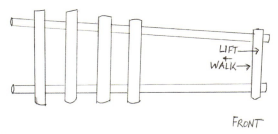

The travois is made with sturdy poles and rope. It's more practical than using a stretcher, but a travois is not recommended to drag a deer, especially if you are out of shape.

A simple way to make a travois is to cut two sturdy ten-foot logs strong enough to hold a deer but not too heavy to drag. Then cut a few shorter poles as cross supports. Test their strength before fastening them with cord to the longer poles. Once the cross supports are fastened tightly, place the deer on the travois. You can also put backpacks and unloaded firearms (that are properly secured) on the travois. Each hunter can grab an end and then work together to drag the deer out. Although it is the better of the pole-carrying methods, it can still be a strenuous ordeal, therefore it is not recommended for older hunters or anyone not in top physical health.

One method that I have seen used many times, particularly by the guides on Anticosti Island, is not only backbreaking but extremely dangerous. It involves a single hunter removing the deer. The guides on Anticosti field dress the deer, then hoist it by themselves over their shoulders and carry it out on their backs. This not only sounds crazy—it actually is. This system requires a lot of psychiatric therapy. It also demands a lot of strength, no regard for getting covered in deer blood, and a total disregard for one's life. Only if you are looking for someone to collect your life insurance should you consider taking a deer out of the woods in this fashion.

A more common way to get deer out of the woods has probably been used by most of you who are reading this. It requires nothing more than grabbing one antler of the buck and dragging it with brute strength. If you're with a buddy, then each hunter grabs an antler and you pull it out together. But here again, there are wiser and safer ways to get your deer out. It should be noted that more hunters are killed by heart attacks using

Photo credit: Fiduccia Enterprises.

My identical twin cousins and long-time hunting companions, Leo and Ralph, are dragging a buck that Ralph (a.k.a. "Junior") shot on his land in upstate New York. They are dragging it the old-fashioned way: by the antlers.

this time-tested dragging method than all the other methods mentioned above (except perhaps the nutty over the shoulder carry-out scheme). I think the over-the-shoulder chaos system kills the hunter from blood dripping into the eyes, causing the hunter to trip with the deer and get impaled by its antlers.

More Practical Extracting Methods

The Homemade Deer Drag: While these deer drag devices work much better than the ones mentioned above, they do have a downside, as dragging a buck using a rope or other type of deer drag can lead to a heart attack. This is particularly true if the hunter is forty-five years or older, and is hunting alone. To fashion a homemade type of deer drag, all the hunter needs is to find a very fresh, stout branch and attach a strong (preferably new) heavy-duty length of rope to it. It is recommended to use a blaze orange vest either to wear or to be attached to the deer. It is better to use this method for short drags over flat ground. It, too, can be dangerous if the hunter trips and falls on rocks and especially on to the antlers.

The Harness Deer Drag: There are many companies that produce shoulder-harness deer drags. These are most useful when the drag will be over longer distances and uneven terrain. There are a wide variety of the shoulder harnesses. I recommend doing your research when considering buying one. The best recommendation I can give you about shoulder-harness deer drags is the old saying: you get what you pay for.

The Pete Rickard Lifetime Deer Drag: The device is made of heavy-duty aircraft cable and has a comfortable, durable rubber handle that is not hard on the hands when dragging longer distances. The cable is easily and quickly slipped around the antlers (or in the case of a doe, around the neck). Simply snug it up a bit, and when you begin dragging the deer, the short length of cable is specifically designed to lift the deer's head and neck off the ground, making for a much easier drag by the hunter.

This drag was originally manufactured by Gotcha Products (a company owned by me and a buddy). We eventually sold it to Pete Rickard, Inc. When we owned the device, we also had a model with two handles that allowed two hunters to drag the deer out, obviously lessening the exertion for each hunter. The Lifetime Deer Drag can genuinely last the lifetime of a hunter. I want to be clear that I don't own this product any longer and I don't know if the Pete Rickard company has made any changes to the device. Like all the rest of the handheld deer drags, do your homework before purchasing one. All dragging devices can cause a heart attack.

I suggest that if any of the following products and/or vehicles are used to extract deer from the field and/or for the road trip home, hunters should use a quality game bag in order to safeguard the meat. A quality game bag will not only help keep off unwanted grime, dust, mud, and anything else, it will also significantly reduce the possibility of insects contaminating the carcass. Additionally, when practical, keep the deer's hide on until you are ready to remove it prior to processing. A game bag over the deer's hide provides a double layer of protection.

Photo credit: Fiduccia Enterprises.

Here I'm using the original Peter Fiduccia Lifetime Deer Drag. The drag has lived up to its name, as the drag I'm using is more than twenty-five years old. It's now called The Lifetime Deer Drag, sold by Pete Rickard, Inc.

Deer Sleds

There are a number of different types of game sleds available. Some are made of flimsy plastic, others of a sturdier plastic, and still others that include various types of plastic materials that are flexible and, to some degree, cloth-like. The downside to all sleds is that, unlike a handheld deer drag, they can be bulky, heavy, and cumbersome to carry into the woods. Often, they are left in an ATV and/or a pickup truck where the hunter can return to get them once the deer is field dressed and ready to be extracted. However, this causes extra work and a loss in time, not to mention the fact that if you are hunting alone, you'll have to leave the deer in the woods until you return for it. Below are some of the more popular deer sleds. I recommend that that you read reviews on the web before purchasing a deer sled.

Magnum Deer Sleigh'r Game Sled by Deer Sleigh'r

According to the manufacturer, "the tough polymer construction of the Sleigh'r sled offers a clean, simple movement of both animals and gear over most terrain. Just strap the game to the sled, thread the included six-foot rope through the grommets, and begin dragging. The sled slides easily over snow, gravel, and light brush; compact and lightweight; protects meat and hide; fits large deer, bear, and elk."

Dead Sled Deer Drag by ARC Products

"The light, effective sled securely hauls game, or can double as a transport for equipment. The versatile twelve-foot tether offers the options of dragging by hand, or configuring it as a chest or waist harness. It is made of high density polyethylene (HDPE) plastic. It includes the sled, three tie-down straps with self-locking steel buckles, and a carrying case." Again, according to the manufacturer.

The Game Sled by Hunting's-A-Drag

I have had personal experience with the Game Sled. It can handle game up to four hundred pounds. According owner Alan Small, creator of the the Game Sled, "Use the handles provided or a tree stand safety belt harness that will not only add more distance between you and the deer, it will also allow for enhanced balance. It comes with its own camo carry bag for easy transport and storage."

Photo credit: Fiduccia Enterprises.

The Game Sled secures deer into the unit, keeping the animal from sliding around or out of the sled. For more info on Game Sleds, go to www.GameSled.com.

The Two-Wheeled Carryalls

Frankly, I have never used a one- or two-wheeled carryall because, in most cases, I don't feel they work well in the steep, rocky terrain that I hunt in the Northeast. Trying to get a deer out of a swamp, or down a steep mountain littered with rocks, boulders, blow downs, stumps, and the like, leaves me wondering about the safety and practicality of their use. As I said, I have no personal experience with using a carryall, so I am only speaking from my mind's eye. I just can't envision taking a 150-pound deer strapped to a carryall down a steep mountain covered in snow or ice. With that said, however, if the land you hunt is mostly flat, slightly hilly, and basically free of major obstructions that may block your route, then I could see the ease, effectiveness, and practical use of them. While I have reservations about using a carryall, that's not to say they are not effective and useful tools even in the type of terrain I mentioned I hunt. I have been told that many hunters find them excellent devices for removing deer.

All varieties of handheld deer drags (sleds, wagons, two-wheel carryalls, etc.) are available at sporting goods stores, online, and in mail-order catalogs including, but not limited to, Bass Pro Shops, Sportsman's Warehouse, Cabela's, Tractor Supply, and Walmart.

ATVs and/or RTVs

Many hunters either own an all-terrain vehicle (ATV) and/or a recreational travel vehicle (RTV). Both make packing a deer out of the woods a safer and easier chore. If the ATV has a rear cargo box, front and rear speed racks, or an attachable utility rack, more than one deer can be taken out at a time. I use my Arctic Cat 700 TBX ATV to get deer out of our woods. It easily and safely negotiates 99 percent of the natural forest and field obstructions commonly found on our property. Almost all ATVs handle this chore well.

When using an ATV/RTV to extract deer, include a game bag to put over the deer. Then place the deer into an ATV bed or tie it to the rack. If you have a buddy nearby, have him/her help you. If you don't have a game bag, an option is to use a tarp in the back of the ATV. Place the deer on top of the tarp and then fold it over the carcass to prevent contaminants from getting into the body cavity. When weather allows, take a gallon of water and some rags to wash out the cavity and the blood off your hands before driving out.

Many companies make these versatile units. Choosing a unit that will perform to your expectations means you should go online and do your homework ahead of time. I have a few Arctic Cat units I use on our land for a wide variety of work, including planting trees, carrying my tools for

Photo credit: Fiduccia Enterprises.

ATVs and RTVs make short work out of removing deer from a majority of different types of terrains. Make sure the deer is securely strapped to the rack or bed of an ATV.

planting food plots, dragging logs, and much more. And I use them regularly for my *most* important task, extracting deer. ATVs have dramatically changed the way deer can be removed from the woods. They not only make the chore a non-issue, but, more important, they help reduce the physical strength needed (and the resulting stress to the body) and add a safety factor when taking a deer from the woods.

The following transport methods include ways to take your deer home once it has been extracted from the woods.

The Bed of a Pickup Truck

Once the deer is removed and brought to the roadside, it can be loaded on or in a vehicle. A convenient way to transport a deer to home, camp, or game pole once it is removed from the field is placing it in the bed of a pickup truck. This is particularly true if the bed is kept clean or at least is covered with a clean tarp before placing the deer in it. The key here is to make sure there is enough circulating air to keep the carcass cool. If the bed is covered, use ice bags to cool the carcass. Place a few large bags of ice in the deer's body cavity for the trip home. If it is a long trip back, place the deer in a quality game bag and pack ice around it. Check to see that the ice remains frozen the entire time. If it doesn't, replace it with new bags along the way.

Of course, not everyone owns a pickup. Still, with a little forethought, practically any vehicle will function sufficiently enough to get your deer home in good condition. Many states still require that a deer carcass, or at least a tagged portion of it, is visible during transport on public highways. On most sedans, the best place is on the roof, especially if you have a roof rack. The trunk is the second-best option.

Photo credit: Fiduccia Enterprises.

The bucks on the back of this pickup truck are heading to our barn, which is a quick trip from the field. The buck in the middle was taken by my wife Kate in 2017.

Again, forethought comes in to play. The best option is to rent or buy a removable roof rack. They are easy to store in the trunk until needed and their length can be adjusted once they are on the roof. The primary advantage of using a roof rack is that they allow the deer to be raised off the car roof. This allows cool air to pass over and underneath the carcass, keeping the deer much cooler during the trip. As a precaution, you can also use a few yards of rope or, better yet, ratchet strap tie downs to further secure the precious load. If the temperature warms up during the trip, place ice bags in the body cavity. Once again, don't take any chances with protecting the quality of your meat.

Vehicle Hitch Carriers

There is no doubt that a rear hitch carrier makes for easy loading, securing, and transport. They can be used on any vehicle or ATV/RTV (with a hitch). My issue with this device is that even when a deer carcass (with hide on) is covered in a game bag, it is still vulnerable to road filth. Even if a tarp is used to protect the meat, the negative effect of that is that it reduces the amount of air circulation and, therefore, cooling. Worse yet, during the entire trip, even on a short haul with an ATV, the meat is exposed to poisonous exhaust fumes. Need I say more? A practical option for vehicle

Photo credit: Discountramps.com

Hitch Carriers can be attached to many types of vehicles. They truly make removing a deer from the woods or taking one home convenient. There are many different designs and models from which to choose.

hitch carriers is to use them to secure gear and/or luggage and then secure the deer carcass on the roof rack stuffed with bags of ice to keep it cool, if need be.

The information in this chapter was included to provide safer and easier ways of bringing a deer out of the field, as well as to reduce physical stress on the successful hunter. It will also possibly reduce the chances of someone having a heart attack when dragging deer out. This information is also meant to help hunters bring home their deer in the best possible condition and get the maximum amount of flavor and tenderness from it.

Photo credit: Fiduccia Enterprises.

Cody and his friends removing his buck from our woods using a Polar trailer. These type of utility trailers attach to ATVs and similar units. They are easy to use and can go wherever your ATV goes. You can find a variety of these units listed at http://stores.clamoutdoors.com/polar-trailer/trailers.html.

Chapter 5

The Essential Guide to Trouble-Free Skinning

Once you have properly field dressed your deer, the next step for better tasting venison is to quickly remove the deer's hide to cool down the meat further. This DIY chapter will demonstrate how to skin a deer using nothing more than a finely honed knife, sharpening steel, small saw, gambrel, and deer hoist. These tools make this task go smoothly.

One of the most annoying elements related to field dressing, skinning, quartering, and butchering deer meat is deer hair. Once a deer is skinned, though, a significant amount of the hair can be removed quickly and easily. Take a small wash cloth and dip it into hot water. Squeeze it out thoroughly. Run the cloth down the carcass in one direction only and then in the opposite way. The damp cloth will pick up the loose hair. Surprisingly it will remove a majority of the hair. Once the cloth gets covered in hair, set it aside and use another clean cloth. Keeping repeating the process as needed. It shouldn't take but a few cloths to remove an overwhelming amount of the hair. To remove any straggling hairs, repeat this process once the deer is quartered and before you butcher it further. Now you are ready to begin skinning the hide from the deer.

Photo credit: Fiduccia Enterprises.

I am caping this bow-killed buck only an hour or so after taking it in a cornfield in Warwick, New York. Within a few short hours after that, I was busy butchering the deer in my kitchen.

The Skinning Process

Skinning Step #1

Start by cutting the hide along the inside of each hind leg. That cut is made from the inside of the skin. Peel the deer's skin and hide over the hind leg to reveal the large tendon at the back of the leg. Carefully slit any connective tissue between the bone and the large tendon. Next, place the end of the gambrel in between the leg bone and the tendon (see photo). Now hoist the carcass to a height that is comfortable to work with.

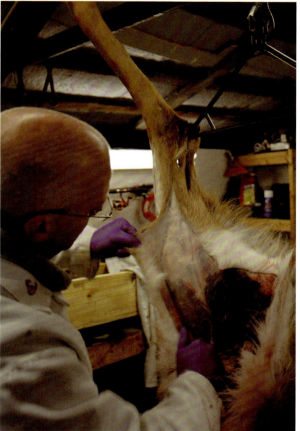

Photo credit: P. Cody Fiduccia.

Our neighbor Darren Hazen makes a hobby of butchering and processing deer. He is an experienced butcher who generally processes a dozen or more deer for family and friends each year in his enclosed wall tent.

Skinning Step #2

With the knife blade turned away from the carcass, cut the hide along the inner side of each leg. Turn the blade back toward the meat and begin skinning the hide around the leg (see insert). Pull hard on the hide with your hands (or with the Game Skinning Tool) once you reach the outside of each leg.

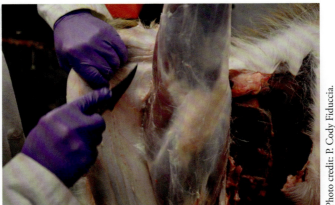

This task is best completed by using a small, super-sharp skinning knife like the "sharp finger" blade model seen here.

Skinning Step #3

With a firm grip, pull the remaining hide down the outside of each leg until the skinned part reaches the deer's tail. Separate the tail as close to the deer's rump as possible. Be careful not to cut into the meat. The tail should remain inside or attached to the hide. Continue skinning the hide along the deer's back by pulling the hide downward with your hand. Slice it free as close to the meat as possible, avoiding cutting into the meat.

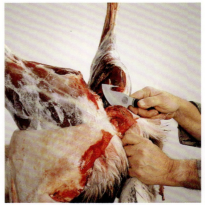

Be careful not to accidentally cut any meat from around this area or the hide, when removing the tail.

Skinning Step #4

Once you reach the middle of the deer's back, grip the hide with both hands and pull it down. Use the tip of your knife blade only when you need to free the hide in places where it catches; again, be extra careful not to slice into or cut off pieces of meat still attached to the hide. Also, be careful not to cut holes in the hide. With your hands, continue to peel the hide down the deer's back and around the rib cage until the hide reaches the front shoulders.

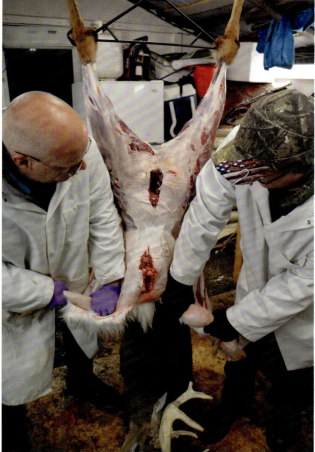

Photo credit: P. Cody Fiduccia.

Darren and his son, Devan, make short work of removing this hide. It's always easier when two people work together on this task.

Skinning Step #5

At this point, cut along the inside of each of the front legs and peel the hide off the front legs. With a stout knife or, better yet, a quality butcher's saw, remove the front legs just above the first joint, which is located above the hooves of the deer.

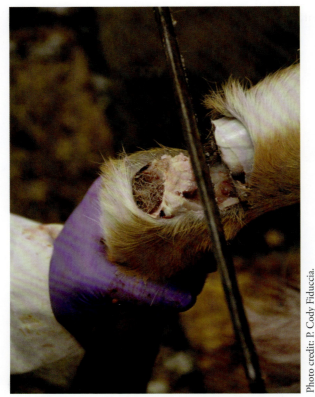

Photo credit: P. Cody Fiduccia.

A quality butcher saw with the right number of teeth will quickly and easily cut through bone. Inexpensive cheap saws generally have blades that wobble or quickly become dull.

Skinning Step #6

Keep pulling, cutting, and peeling the hide as far down the deer's neck as possible. Once you have pulled the hide to the lowest point on the neck, cut the deer's head free of the body with a butcher's meat saw. The more neck meat you save, the better stew or ground venison you will have. Once the hide is removed, spread it out on a clean, flat surface with the hair facing down. Scrape off any remaining pieces of fat, tallow, meat, or blood. The hide is ready to be salted if it is going to be preserved or brought to the taxidermist for tanning (unless you do your own tanning).

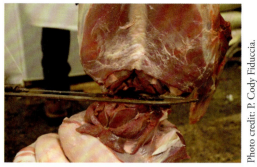

Photo credit: P. Cody Fiduccia.

When removing the head from the carcass, cut as close to the head as possible in order to save as much meat as you can. Neck meat makes excellent stew or can be put into ground venison.

After the Hide is Removed

After the hide is removed, inspect the carcass for meat that may have been damaged by a bullet or broadhead. Some bloodshot meat looks a lot worse than it really is, so inspect it carefully. Contrary to popular belief, bloodshot

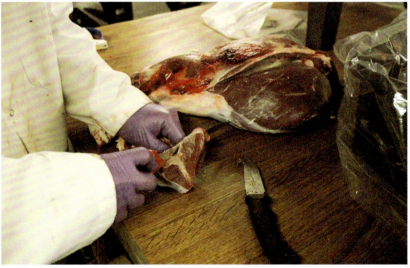

Photos Credit: Fiduccia Enterprises.

Don't discard bloodshot meat without first inspecting it closely. Many times, it looks worse than it is and is actually salvageable. Be sure to trim anything that looks discolored or slimy.

meat can often be salvaged. Remove the section that is blood shot and trim away any slime, fat, connective tissue, blood, or other destroyed meat. Once you have done this, put the bloodshot section in the refrigerator to let it chill down. When cooled, it will be easier to see and remove any additional blood-soaked areas that were missed.

Some butchers feel that the meat should soak overnight in salt water in a refrigerator (or, if the ambient room temperature is between 32 and 37 degrees, it may be left on a butcher table). After the meat has soaked overnight, remove it from the liquid, and thoroughly blot it dry. This process will clean bloodshot meat sufficiently enough to use for ground, stew, or sausage meat. It doesn't pay to try to save bloodshot meat that is extensively damaged or pieced by bone from bullet damage, however.

Helpful Tips

- It is much easier to skin a deer or any game soon after it is killed. The hide will peel off quickly and effortlessly. This is much easier than having to strain to pull the skin off days later, when the carcass is cold.
- The quickest and easiest way to remove the hide without pulling your back out or straining your arms is to use a hide removal tool.
- To make the job of skinning more comfortable, hang the deer using a pulley (or, better yet, an electric hoist) so you can raise or lower the deer to eye level without straining.
- To avoid accidentally removing usable pieces of meat, regularly hone your knife with a sharpening steel while skinning.
- During all skinning cuts, keep the knife blade pointed outward to avoid cutting deer hair.
- When you are ready to remove the deer tail, cut the tail bone from the underside, and the tail will remain on the hide.

Chapter 6

A Step-by-Step Manual to Quartering

Generally speaking, it is probably safe to say that a lot of hunters begin butchering right after the deer is skinned. My problem with this is that butchering a hanging deer into smaller cuts is not as safe as butchering a quartered carcass that is on a table. Whether a deer is fabricated into smaller cuts while it is hanging or it is quartered and then cut up into smaller cuts, is up to the individual hunter. In both instances, though, it is handy to have an extra hand to provide some help. If you plan to quarter the deer first, which is what I recommend, know that a deer's front leg can easily weigh fifteen to twenty pounds, and the back leg is heavier. So, it also becomes a safety issue when you remove a leg and try to brace it while holding a knife.

With a little know-how, you can easily learn to quarter your deer, though it might seem a daunting task at first. To make this a convenient and an enjoyable project, you'll need to know the portions of the deer with which you will be working.

Many folks believe that quartering a deer at home involves a lot more work and tools, as well as taking a long time, and requires a large working area. In reality, none of these points are true. All the tools you need to get the job done quickly and easily are a quality knife, sharpening steel, and small butcher's meat saw. With a little know-how, anyone can remove a deer's forequarters and hindquarters, tenderloins, ribs, and backstraps at home by following these simple step-by-step directions.

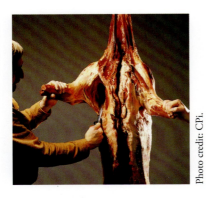

Photo credit: CPi.

Quartering Step #1

Begin by using a sharp hunting or butchering knife and push the front leg away from the deer's skinned carcass. Place the knife with the sharp edge down and cut the connective meat and tissue free from between the leg and the rib cage. Continue cutting through this section until you reach the shoulder. As mentioned above, the process is safer and easier if someone holds the carcass securely while you cut the foreleg free. If you don't have help available, another option is to tie the opposite leg to an anchor point to steady the carcass.

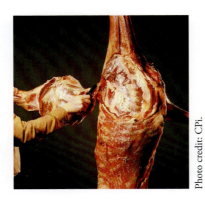

Photo credit: CPi.

Quartering Step #2

Remove the front leg at the point where it reaches the shoulder by cutting between the shoulder blade and the back. Repeat steps one and two on the opposite front leg. Once both legs are off, remove the layer of brisket meat that is located over the deer's ribs. This is ideal meat for stew, ground, or sausage.

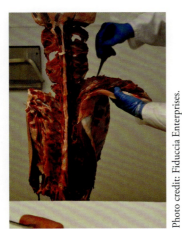

Photo credit: Fiduccia Enterprises.

Quartering Step #3

Now, cut the meat at the base of the neck, which will enable you to cut the backstrap free. With your knife blade facing down and the tip of the blade pressed closely to the bone, guide the knife slowly down toward the rump of the deer. Be extra careful not to cut into the prized backstraps, to avoid leaving any of its prime meat behind. The two backstraps lie on each side of the spine. I prefer to butterfly the backstraps into steaks or pound them into thinner cutlets. They can also be sliced very thinly for sautéing, one of the more flavorful ways to cook them. Once you have reached the rump area, you can cut off the backstrap.

Quartering Step #4

Next, cut one of the hind legs off to expose the ball-and-socket joint. Separate the joint by forcefully pushing the leg backward until the joint pops apart. Now cut through the joint. Carefully work your knife around the tailbone and pelvis area until the leg is totally free. Repeat this step on the opposite rear leg.

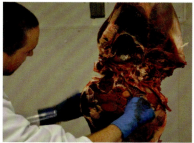

Photo credit: Fiduccia Enterprises.

Quartering Step #5

After trimming away the flank meat below the last rib, you can begin to cut the tenderloins from the inside of the deer's body cavity.

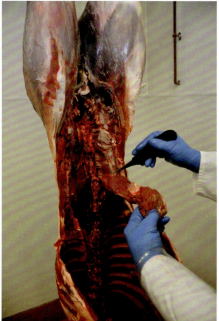

Photo credit: Fiduccia Enterprises.

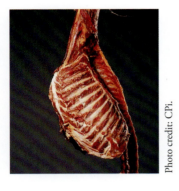

Photo credit: CPi.

Quartering Step #6

To remove the ribs, simply saw along the backbone of the deer. Cut around the base of the neck and then snap off the backbone. Set aside the neck and head. Carefully bone out as much useable meat from the neck as possible—it makes terrific ground meat and/or can be used for sausage.

Quartering Step #7

Photo credit: CPi.

To enhance the flavor of the ribs, carefully cut away the ridge of meat and gristle on the bottom of the ribs. This will leave you with a trimmed section of ribs to work with. Cut the ribs into racks of four to six pieces. If you want to make the ribs into short ribs, saw them in half. If you prefer not to eat the ribs, don't discard them. Instead, bone the meat from the ribs and grind it into sausage or burger meat.

Now that you are done, you will have two forelegs, two hind legs, two backstraps, two tenderloins, and two sets of ribs.

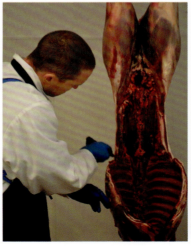

Photo credit: Fiduccia Enterprises.

Did You Know?

- Flank meat is often used to make jerky. The flank cut can also be used to grind up for burger meat.

- By removing the tenderloins before properly aging your deer, you will prevent the tenderloins from turning black and dehydrating. Removing them before aging the meat will dramatically increase their taste and essence.

- The primary cause of bad-tasting game meat is from not removing as much of the silver skin, or the shiny, slimly looking connective tissue, and tallow from the meat as possible. This is how venison becomes gamy. Removing every piece of tallow is a time-consuming process. It is worth the effort to get the best tasting wild game, however. Fat from domestic animals imparts a tasty flavor to the meat. That is definitely not the case with wild animals, particularly antlered game.

- To test the tenderness of various cuts, pinch a small piece of each primary cut between your thumb and forefinger. At first, meat that is not tender will offer resistance. As you continue to apply pressure, the meat will dimple slightly. Tender cuts, however, will give more easily when pinched. If too much pressure is applied, the meat will become softer to the touch.

Chapter 7

Facts about Properly Aging Venison

Once a deer is properly field dressed and the carcass has cooled correctly, there are two options to choose from in regard to aging the meat. Meat can either be aged as wet or dry for several days or you can butcher it. Most deer are killed between 1½ and 2½ years old. For instance, most male deer killed in my home state of New York are only 1½ years old. Unless deer live in dire conditions, and have limited food sources, the meat from a majority of 1½ to 2½-year-olds can be considered as prime venison. I have, and I am sure many of you have, also taken 3½- and 4½-year-old deer with meat that was tasty and tender.

This yearling deer is typical for a majority of the deer shot in New York. Dr. Victor Schultz, a member of the Nerd Gang, holds a PhD in Organic Synthetic Chemistry. The deer was Victor's first buck. As per hunting rules for our farm, Victor now can only take an 8-point buck or better.

Therefore, unless you would like to test whether aging will further enhance the tenderness of your deer's meat, you may want to skim over this chapter. Or, at least, pass the information on dry aging and, instead, concentrate on the wet-aging section.

Dry Aging

Let's discuss the practicality of properly aging a deer or other big game animal. In order to age (tenderize) venison and even domestic beef, specific guidelines must be followed. As previously mentioned, there are two different methods to aging deer meat or other wild game meat. The first is commonly referred to as dry aging. During dry aging, the enzyme activity breaks down connective tissues that cause the meat to be tough.

Photo credit: Fiduccia Enterprises.

These sides of beef are hanging in a 38°F cooler. In order to properly dry age domestic beef and/or wild venison, controlled temperature, humidity, and air flow guidelines must be followed.

There are very few hunters who butcher their own deer who have the required cooling facilities to properly dry age venison. Dry aging is the method whereby a deer is stored in a refrigerated cooler at a consistent temperature between 34°F and 36°F (temperatures above 40°F promote bacterial growth), with a relative humidity at approximately 85 to 95 percent and about twenty feet of air flow constantly blowing across the meat. It should become crystal clear that the old advice to hang a deer outside for an inordinate amount of time in varying temperatures and weather conditions is absolutely not the way to age deer properly. Instead, it tenderizes the meat because it begins to decay—yuck. Another one of my pet peeves about hanging your deer outside is that it also invites a host of insects, including the always filthy, disgusting flies that lay their eggs within your meat. Need I say more?

On average, a majority of meat experts suggest a venison carcass should usually age for about seven to ten days. Under the above ideal conditions, however, I believe five days is plenty of time to achieve proper aging (I'll explain why below). It becomes easy to see that unless a hunter has a friend or professional butcher with a cooler or a budget that can afford a portable or stand-alone walk-in cooler that is capable of providing these conditions, the reality of properly dry aging venison at home diminishes significantly.

For those DIY butchers who want to take their home butchering to the maximum level, there is an option to consider. At this writing, a company called Koola Buck makes two different portable walk-in

Photo credit: Koolabuck.com.

For a variety of DIY butchering reasons, owning a portable cooler like this Koola Buck Pro4 will help you take your deer butchering to the next level. For more information on portable coolers, visit Koolabuck.com.

coolers. These units, which are not inexpensive, can be set up and broken down in ten minutes or so. They function well to keep your deer meat cool, reducing the possibility of the meat being spoiled by warm weather. They can also be used for those hunters who want to "age" venison. They are especially helpful for those who hunt deer in warmer climates. For more information, visit www.koolabuck.com.

Hide On, Hide Off

If it is practical to age your venison as described above, one element to be taken into consideration is whether to leave the deer's hide on or off during the time it is left to hang in the cooler. During the aging process, no matter which way you dry age the venison—hide on or hide off—moisture will be lost. If the hide is left on the deer, the meat will lose minimal moisture. Wild game has a very thin layer of fat (compared to beef). So, if the hide is removed during dry aging, the loss of moisture can be up to 20 percent and a greater amount of dried meat will have to be trimmed off. For me, the answer has always been to leave the hide on, as that lets you recover every possible ounce of venison.

Wet Aging

The other method to age venison is called wet aging. Wet aging is a process where meat that has been vacuum-packed (or shrink-wrapped), and from which all oxygen has been removed, sits in a refrigerator to age for a few weeks. With wet aging, it is not necessary to control the humidity or the air flow around the meat. Because this involves vacuum packing, it is often done with smaller cuts of meat, yet not necessarily packaged in portion sizes. This is a much more practical method and less expensive way (because you don't have to buy or find a temperature- and humidity-controlled cooler) to age deer meat. Generally, wet aging only takes a few days to tenderize the meat. However, this method is best achieved if the home butcher has a small refrigerator dedicated for this purpose. It just isn't practical to think you can age a lot of meat in the family refrigerator.

Again, the home butcher must decide if the process of aging venison (dry or wet) is worth the effort. As long as the processing of the deer is done

Photo credit: Mike Ring.

In order to wet age meat correctly, it must first be vacuum packed properly and then left in a refrigerator for a few weeks.

correctly, from the instant the deer was quickly killed to the final stages of butchering, the meat should be both tender and flavorful. If, on the other hand, the deer was stressed prior to it being shot, or wounded, or not properly cared for from the field to when it was butchered, then aging can certainly help tenderize the meat.

One element that is often overlooked regarding taking care of an animal that was just killed is removing it from the woods and getting it back to camp or home. As mentioned in chapter 4 on getting your deer home, many hunters don't even stop to think that putting your deer onto the back of a vehicle (or even on the back of a dirty ATV) without properly protecting it with a game bag (or some other cover) while transporting negatively affects the meat. No amount of aging will help cure poor care of a deer from field to table. I often tell people that they should treat recently killed deer as they would if they bought an expensive beef steer (remember what Jim said in chapter 4 about this?).

Additionally, it should be noted that if you are going to use a good portion of your meat as ground, stew meat, jerky, or sausage, you can skip the process of aging entirely. If you prefer not to age your deer, dry or wet, you should wait at least twenty-four hours before butchering it. This will give the carcass time to cool and the muscles time to relax. If this advice is not taken, I can assure you that the meat will be tough while the muscles are still contracted.

DIY home butchers who use most of the venison as ground, stew, jerky, or sausage don't have to be concerned with dry and/or wet aging their venison.

Photo credit: Mike Ring.

Chapter 8

Enclosed Butchering Work Areas

Before a hunter commits to undertake the DIY project of home butchering, he or she should consider the value and usefulness of butchering deer in an enclosed protected area. An enclosed protected area is strongly suggested if you intend to get more deeply involved with home butchering on a long-term basis. Any well-planned, enclosed work area will have sources of:

- light
- electricity
- enough comfortable space to work in
- clean water (even a clean five-gallon bucket will do)
- a source of controlled temperature (Note: While the work area should be comfortable enough to work in without wearing a jacket, the temperature must be cool enough not to spoil the meat. This is true of all enclosed areas used to butcher meat.)

The options for an enclosed area can include a dedicated shed, roomed-off space in a garage, small outbuilding, wall tent, dedicated walled-off area in a home basement, or even a temporary home kitchen area. Using a home kitchen to butcher deer can be somewhat problematic, particularly if your spouse doesn't share your passion about butchering dead deer in the house.

Photo credit: Fiduccia Enterprises.

This shed will make an ideal space to butcher deer. My cousins and I thoroughly cleaned the interior in preparation for putting in all our butchering equipment. A benefit of having a shed behind your home is that you can run water to the building.

With that noted, if your spouse hunts, using the kitchen to butcher deer is one of the best choices to consider. Your kitchen will provide all the comforts, including running water, sturdy and comfortable work areas, electricity, adjustable temperatures, and much more.

There are several considerations for establishing an enclosed area in which to butcher your deer. Each has its own benefits and tradeoffs. I can guarantee you that having an enclosed area will greatly enhance your comfort, save time and money, improve the overall quality and flavor of the meat, and greatly reduce the possibility of meat contamination. Enclosed butchering areas should be considered just another butchering "tool" by the DIY home butcher.

Any enclosed butchering areas should be entirely dedicated to that chore. The possible choices are listed in the order of my preference. Although each choice offers similar elements, there are important differences with each, ranging from their cost to conveniences each provides. All the choices below except the home kitchen should include a wood or fabric door that can be locked to keep children out.

- A home kitchen
- A twelve-by-twelve-foot or larger shed with a locking door
- A walled-off area with a locking door in a home basement and/or garage
- A wall tent with a sturdy wood floor and a door and/or zippered flap that can be locked
- A clean existing outbuilding
- A walled-off area in a clean barn (that isn't used to house animals)

Home Kitchen

Photo credit: Kate Fiduccia.

There's no doubt that butchering your deer in a home kitchen will be the most comfortable, the cleanest, and the best equipped area.

It has been my experience over the last five decades that a kitchen with sufficient space is *the* top choice for butchering deer at home. It already has electricity, water, heat (that will have to be kept at a lower than normal level during the butchering process), and, most likely, enough space in which to work comfortably. It will be the most hygienic and convenient area of all the choices. Even the cleanup will be much easier and quicker than the other choices mentioned above. There are several downsides to consider, however, when choosing to use the kitchen. The first is that the skinning and quartering of the deer will still have to be someplace else:

- in a clean space in an unfinished home basement
- a clean area of a home garage or shed
- or even under a game pole (hopefully with a roof to shield the deer and the hunter from foul weather)

Once the deer is skinned and about to be quartered, each quarter should be kept cool even when it is brought inside to be butchered. This will mean lowering the temperature in your home while you are butchering your deer. Also, to prevent blood from dripping on the floors when taking the quarters back to the kitchen, wrap each quarter in a small tarp.

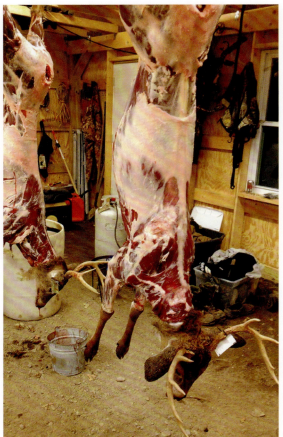

Photo credit: Mike Ring.

These deer are hanging in a dedicated shed built for butchering deer. Recently skinned, they are going to be quartered and then broken down into smaller cuts.

The next complication with butchering deer in the kitchen depends on how many people live in the house. The kitchen can be a busy room, particularly if there are children looking for meals or snacks. A home kitchen can end up being problematic in this case, especially so if the family is larger than four people. Then you can count on a lot of interruptions, which can complicate the process. On the other hand, if you live alone or just with your spouse, then the kitchen is by far the best choice.

Walled-Off Basement Area

Photo credit: Fiduccia Enterprises.

I built a twelve-by-twelve-foot room in the basement of our longtime home in Warwick, New York as a dedicated area to butcher deer.

This is another good option. But for it to work most efficiently and to keep it out of the way of all the other family members using it, it should be walled-off and have a door that can be locked. It can provide many of the features a kitchen area will, including a small wash-sink for water. It can have a controlled heat source and the concrete floor can be easily cleaned.

Walled-Off Garage Area

If you have a large enough space in an attached garage and it is not overcrowded with other things stored there, it may offer another spot to build

Photo credit: Fiduccia Enterprises.

For a very affordable price in materials and labor, a room for butchering deer can be constructed in an attached garage with ample space.

an enclosed, lockable room to butcher your deer. While it has all the advantages a walled-off basement room has, it does have a notable negative. It probably houses a vehicle or two. To prevent odors of gasoline and carbon monoxide getting into the butchering area, vehicles should not be stored in the garage when processing game. Also be sure to ventilate the area thoroughly before butchering the deer. Again, it should have a door with a sturdy lock.

New Shed

If you have the outdoor space, it might be a more practical choice to build or buy a shed. It can be as small as twelve by twelve or even larger. It is important that the shed be placed on a well-prepared section of *leveled ground.* Generally, the plywood flooring in store-bought sheds always needs to be reinforced. Depending on the budget, you can use either one-half or three-quarter-inch exterior plywood to be screwed down over the existing floor. This will sturdy-up the building considerably and allow the storage of more heavy equipment in the shed as well. Regarding store-bought sheds, another helpful tip is that you should reinforce the section of the rafters

Photo credit: Fiduccia Enterprises.

A prebuilt shed is convenient and a quick way to have a place to butcher deer. By walking through different models, you'll be able to decide the space that will work best for your butchering needs.

where you will hang the deer carcass. By strengthening the rafters, you are assured that you can hang and work on heavy game safely. If it isn't realistic to bring in piped water, try to locate the shed someplace on the property near a source of water. You can insulate a garden hose in order to bring a reliable source of water into the shed during the cold winter months.

If at all practical and affordable, run electric to the shed. That will be a huge plus. Otherwise, use a heavy-duty exterior extension cord hooked up to an outside source of electricity or an inexpensive generator (I have a portable generator that was only $150 at Tractor Supply). The extension cord can be plugged into a multiple six-outlet power strip or, if the generator is capable, use an industrial power eight-outlet power strip. With this, you can run a couple of small electric heaters set low enough to keep the meat cool, but also comfortable enough to work in.

If needed, particularly in a larger enclosed space, a small Mr. Heater (or two) kept on low and properly ventilated near a window will work too. Another inexpensive heating option is to install a very small wood stove (available at Lowes and Home Depot for $100, not counting in the pipes and so on) to warm the building. When using a wood stove, however, you must be extra careful not to allow it to be stoked with too much wood or it will *overheat* the area while the meat is being processed. If you use a wood stove in a confined area like a shed, it can quickly turn the shed into a sauna. It should be kept at a temperature that takes the chill out of the air but not much more than that. It should not be used during the process of "aging" your deer prior to breaking it down. I like a wood stove because I use it to warm water to periodically clean knives and saws as I work, and the warm water makes the cleanup process easier. What is also unique about a dedicated enclosed area, even more than a home kitchen, is that it can be stocked with a variety of butchering tools and appliances (grinders, vats, tubs, electric meat saws, etc.) as well as a lot of other butchering equipment, making everything at the ready and handy at an arm's reach away when you want to butcher a deer.

Wall Tent

Photo credit: Fiduccia Enterprises.

A wall tent, like this one owned by our friend Darren Hazen, is a viable option for butchering game. In many cases, they are more affordable than most prebuilt sheds.

Wall tents can be used not only at remote deer camp; they are also a good option for butchering deer at home. There are countless shapes, sizes, and prices from which to choose. My three favorite styles are Guide tents, Arctic Hoop tents, and after-market military tents. Most times, wall tents are quite affordable as well. For instance, a ten-foot by twelve-foot canvas aluminum framed tent can be purchased for about $500 to $700. Some even come with stove pipe shields, windows, and are mildew resistant. Most come only with canvas floors, however. But, by placing four-foot by eight-foot by three-quarter-inch sheets of exterior plywood over the canvas floor, hunters can easily create a sturdy floor that will hold more weight. Many of the

Photo credit: P. Cody Fiduccia.

Darren Hazen gets ready to remove the hide of a deer in his wall tent. Wall tents can be equipped with heaters, electricity, and water, making them convenient enclosed places for butchering deer.

military-style tents can be purchased new or used. The more traditional guide and/or hoop tents are available at all the big box sporting goods stores, including Cabela's, Bass Pro Shops, Dick's, Gander Outdoors, and Sportsman's Guide. If you consider a wall tent, do your research, as there are myriads of choices, prices, options, styles, and qualities. Similar to sheds, tents also require being placed on well-prepared leveled ground.

If you decide on a tent, the only option for water is to either have an insulated hose (so the hose doesn't freeze up in November and December) close enough to reach the tent. More than likely, if you want electric in the tent, a well-ventilated outside generator will be the most practical option. The best heating source for a wall tent will be an inexpensive small wood stove. Again, don't allow the stove to overheat the tent area for any length of time while the meat is being processed or aged.

With a wall tent, like a shed, you can have a wood stove in it and warm up water to clean knives and saws, and also use for cleanup. Wall tents provide an enclosed area to stock a variety of butchering tools and appliances (grinder, vats, tubs, professional electric meat saws, etc.) as well as other butchering equipment, making everything easily available while you work.

Existing Outbuilding

If you have an outbuilding on your property that is not being used, but is structurally sound and can be well cleaned, it can be converted into an area to do your home butchering. It will provide many of the benefits a new shed will, but it saves a lot of money from having to purchase a new shed or wall tent.

Barn Space

The caveat of this choice is that the barn area must be clean and have no animals living in it. If it is clean and animal-free, like a home basement area it must still be walled-off, have a door that locks, and is much cleaner than the rest of the barn. This area has many of the same benefits of a walled-off garage area. Additionally, if the barn has an existing water source, a small wash sink can be installed.

Photo credit: Mike Ring.

This small barn is used by avid DIY butcher Mike Ring and his equally ardent butchering friends. This space is used only for butchering game and is kept clean. While it does have a dirt floor, there is always the option to put a wood or concrete floor over it.

Some Final Thoughts on Your Butcher Shop

With the exception of a home kitchen, all of the other options should have doors that can be locked to keep children out. A home butchering area contains a lot of knives and other equipment that can be dangerous in young hands. Other than the home kitchen, all the other areas need to be kept as free as possible of rodents, insects, and foul odors. Even fabric tents have doors and they, too, should be locked. When any area (other than the kitchen) is in use, keep it well ventilated, particularly if you are using some type of heat source, a generator, and/or strong fluids used to clean up.

I can assure you of this, though: If you are serious about getting involved in long-term DIY home butchering of deer, if your "butcher shop" work area has warmth, adequate light, water, a comfortable working space, and it fits your other equipment without overcrowding, you will be butchering deer comfortably for many years to come. Therefore, if you don't use the kitchen, it is totally worth making a small investment to achieve the goal of securing a sanitary, enclosed room or building. A comfortable enclosed work area ends up being a tool, one of the most important tools a hunter can have in order to be a proficient DIY home butcher. It will also provide years of enjoyment and self-satisfaction! Think of a dedicated area to butcher your deer as a primary DIY butchering tool.

One last thought about your butcher shop. Don't be tempted to store any type of equipment other than your butchering paraphernalia in there. If the enclosure has electric, keep all appliances (grinders, slicers, heaters, etc.) unplugged when they are not in use. This should go without saying, but since I have witnessed some people doing it, I will mention it: NEVER store any gasoline or equipment filled with gasoline in a structure, particularly in an enclosed area where you intend to butcher venison. Sounds crazy for a wide variety of reasons, right? However, I have seen it done.

Chapter 9

Butchering at Deer Camp

I covered my thoughts about butchering deer in clean, comfortable, and convenient enclosed locations (kitchens, sheds, etc.) in an earlier chapter. But let's face it, in some cases, deer and other big game may have to be butchered at camp. When I use the term *deer camp,* it is meant to encompass a varied description of different types of amenities and conveniences available at hunting camps and what they offer in the way of butchering deer. Some are nothing more than base tents used to hunt from. Generally, in these cases, bagged deer or other big game are hung on trees or makeshift meat poles and are then skinned, quartered, and butchered outside. Another description of a deer camp would be anything from a one-room cabin, a motorhome, pickup camper, or, perhaps, a more conventional cabin with a couple of rooms with a generator, a water source, and hopefully an indoor toilet rather than an outhouse. These types of deer camps are most often off the beaten trail and make the entire project of processing deer more of a chore. This point alone is a determining factor how a deer killed at camp ends up having its meat butchered. The most important factor when hunting out of a deer camp is to keep a deer carcass as clean as possible as it is being broken down and butchered into the different cuts of meat.

In any of the above type camps, most often the hunter has no choice but to hang and butcher the entire deer outside (when a deer is hung outside, if at all possible, hang the deer in a shaded area). Begin the process by removing the hide and begin breaking down the carcass into smaller cuts that can be butchered on a sturdy kitchen table, picnic bench, or work counter. Or, cut off quarters and butcher the deer in a tent or cabin. Since

Photo credit: Fiduccia Enterprises.

When a deer is hung outside, try to place it in a shaded area to help keep the carcass cool, particularly in the early part of the season. This deer is hanging from a leafless oak tree, but is shaded by the large pines behind it.

weather conditions can vary, your first decision to preserve the quality of your meat is to, as soon as possible, cover the deer with a game bag and begin to break the carcass down into primal cuts (four legs, spine with backstraps intact, and the neck).

It is often recommended to hang a deer at camp at least a day before butchering it. I can see the value in this (weather permitting), as the extra time helps the carcass to drain itself of any leftover body fluids. It also provides the opportunity for hunters to make any additional cleaning of the carcass. If the weather is cold enough, it helps to firm up the meat, which will make for easier cutting. A point to consider when a deer is hanging at camp is that you don't want it to hang in frigid weather more than a day because you will end up with a frozen carcass. This is no easy way to deal with cutting meat. Venison that has been butchered from a carcass that is frozen solid will have considerably reduced flavor and tenderness.

My main concern with any deer hanging outside, however, is that the carcass is vulnerable to infestation from insects, particularly blowflies. This is a factor that is rarely talked about in detail by many butchering experts. I believe they avoid it because of the reality of how badly the meat can become infested with insect larvae. I disagree. I think every hunter should be made aware of the critical importance of protecting their deer meat as thoroughly as possible to avoid this situation. Common houseflies do enough damage, but the hellish red-eyed monster known as the blowfly will do the most damage as it lays thousands of tiny white eggs throughout the meat. I know I have mentioned it several times before. But, when you stop to think about what insect larvae can do to the meat you are about to eat, it is worth repeating several times.

Another disgusting infesta-tion to hanging deer and other big game meat occurs when a variety of birds, including pigeons, peck at the meat while pooping all over it! The best insurance you can use to prevent blowflies, other insects, and birds from using your deer carcass as a depository for eggs to hatch, or as a meat market and outdoor toilet, is to cover the carcass with a quality game bag, properly used as directed.

Photo credit: Pond5.

Many types of flies (house fly, botfly, and bot-tle fly) are germ-infested insects. Like this red-eyed monster, they'll lay thousands of revolting eggs in a deer carcass, providing the disgusting larvae a dining area once they hatch.

Here is a key factor to consider when purchasing a quality game bag: The inexpensive (cheap) one- or two-dollar cheesecloth game bags will not do the job well. This is because the mesh is too wide and is ineffective in preventing blowflies and other egg-laying insects from contacting the meat. Spend the extra money and buy heavy-duty game bags. They are porous, but the mesh is tightly woven and made from either cotton or muslin. They are several times more expensive than cheap game bags. However, they will do the job several times better than the cheaper game bags and can be re-used for many deer seasons.

Photo credit: Fiduccia Enterprises.

To significantly reduce the chance of insect infestation, like larger botflies, use a quality game bag with a tightly woven mesh. Better yet, use a Koola Buck antimicrobial game bag such as the one pictured in this photo.

When at camp, if the weather is cold enough, insects are much less of an issue, but still a concern. If the weather is warm, however, I strongly recommend letting the covered deer (in a game bag) hang no more than overnight and that you begin the butchering process as early as possible the following day. This is very important, as research has proven that the two leading elements that cause countless pounds of venison to be lost are warm weather and vermin infestation. Another consideration is that the carcass should not be subjected to fluctuating temperatures that are so varied that they drop below 20°F at night and go higher than 45°F during the day.

If this occurs, take immediate steps to prevent the meat from freezing or becoming too warm. Covering the carcass with a tarp can help prevent it from freezing overnight.

Butchering deer in camp basically breaks down to being prepared with at least the most basic tools, equipment, and makeshift work areas. This option is not *my* first choice, but again, in deer camp, most times the options are limited due to the remoteness of the camp. Taking that into consideration, the basic tools that will be needed in camp include a hoist, gambrel, game bag, a skinning and boning knife, handsaw (with extra blades), and sharpening steel.

Other items should include a large, quality, insulated cooler or two and butcher paper and tape for wrapping cuts of meat. With today's technology, even at a remote hunting camp, you can bring a battery-operated vacuum sealer with plastic vacuum bags instead of butcher paper. With either, you should have a sufficient amount of dry ice. A note of caution about using dry ice is that any time it is enclosed in a cooler or chest, it will emit gas (carbon dioxide) as the ice transforms, and that must be occasionally vented. Intermittently opening the cover of the cooler for a few seconds will solve this issue. You will also need a sturdy table or workbench. When the time comes to cut meat in camp, most often it is done on a table in the cabin, or in the worst case, on a picnic table or a piece of plywood secured on two wooden horses. In any of the above cases, be sure to have a large synthetic cutting board to cut the meat on. It will also be easier to clean with water and/or a bleach-water solution.

When practical, at deer camp, and especially at a more remote type of camp, my best advice is to only break the deer carcass down into quarters and then take it home to butcher further. By breaking the whole carcass down into the primal cuts (front and rear legs, saddle, and neck), it will be easier to put into iced-down coolers (or coolers packed with dry ice). It is also not necessary at camp to be overly fussy about trimming the smaller cuts of meat, including the tenderloins, backstraps, ribs, and so on. That can be done once the carcass is at home. For deer killed in a remote camp, another option is to cool the carcass overnight and, if at all possible, take it to the closest processing place to have it quartered (while you are there to watch it). Then, take the quarters, place them in iced-down coolers, and take them home to break them down into the finer cuts. It is better to leave camp early in order to ensure your venison will be excellent tablefare, than have it end up being less tender and flavorful, or worse, spoiled.

Additional Camp Tips

- After the deer is killed, it is crucial to field dress it as safely and quickly as possible in order to allow the body heat to dissipate quickly.
- At camp, most deer are hung from trees or meat poles. Make sure the carcass is hung high so that predators like coyotes or bears can't reach it easily.
- At a remote deer camp, always bring a light block and tackle with opposing pulleys to hoist the deer high onto a sturdy branch.
- Having a few well-built quality coolers at camp goes a long way to keeping your prized venison arriving at home in tip-top tablefare condition.
- When flying home with deer meat in coolers, it is vital to make sure each cooler is marked "Perishable Meat." The cooler/s should be wrapped tightly and securely with tape.
- In the case of a delayed or cancelled flight, be aware that most airports have freezer facilities and are prepared to store coolers if need be. (Sometimes there is an added charge for the service.)
- If your flight is cancelled and you have to stay overnight somewhere, try to select a large hotel with a restaurant. They have walk-in coolers for food storage, and most will allow their guests to store their meat in their walk-in coolers. I have done both of these things when returning with moose meat from Newfoundland.

Photo credit: Fiduccia Enterprises.

These two products go a long way with helping eliminate a majority of one of the least thought about, but most problematic issues with a deer carcass—insect infestation. www.koolabuck.com.

Chapter 10

The Butchering Groups

There are basically four groups of hunters who home butcher their deer: those who butcher deer out of necessity; those who butcher at camp/home outdoors; the DIY butcher; and lastly, the professional butcher.

The Necessity Butcher

This first group consists of hunters who may lack the extra disposable funds to take their deer to a processing plant. Or, they may live in such rural areas that traveling or even finding a processing plant close by is not an option. This group gets the job done (usually hanging their deer out of doors with a rope from a stout tree limb) by using a bare minimum of butchering tools, most often with nothing more than a single hunting knife and a handsaw.

Photo credit: Fiduccia Enterprises.

Although I customarily hung, skinned, and quartered my deer outside for many years, I always brought the carcasses inside to butcher them.

The Outdoor Butcher

The second faction of hunters might be the largest of the four groups, at least for now. They are the hunters who butcher their game, again usually outside, at deer camp or even at home. For countless years hunters have hung their deer on an unroofed game pole, sturdy tree branch, or even from under a deck at home. Some of them, mostly the old-timers, hang their deer for extended periods of time prior to butchering because they still believe that hanging deer outside for a prolonged amount of time is the best way to age (cure) deer and other game meat. I absolutely assure you that it is not. I'll address exactly why in a later chapter.

From whereever the deer is hung, they skin it and break it down into quarters. Then, taking one quarter at time, they begin to butcher it, most often on a wobbly table outside. While butchering their deer, they routinely are forced to tolerate and brave all types of weather, from extremely cold to unusually warm, to get the job done.

This technique works, but it has many flaws. Not only do these hunters put up with bad weather, but they also risk contaminating the meat and allowing flying insects, birds, bugs, and other vermin access to a fresh food source. More disgustingly, this method also allows for an enticing place for insects to lay their eggs. The eggs are white and are about 1.2mm in length (making them difficult to detect).

More troublesome, within a day the larvae (maggots) will hatch and immediately begin to feed on (usually dead and decaying) organic material, such as carrion, feces, garbage, and/or the deer meat they laid their eggs in.

This segment of hunters does use a few more tools than the first group does, however. Their tools usually include a couple of all-purpose knives (most times it's their hunting knives), a meat hand saw, a knife sharpener of some type, and a gambrel. After bringing a quarter to the less-than-stable

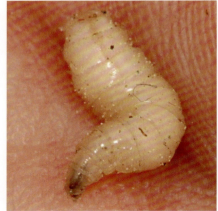

Photo credit: Something's Crawling in My Hair.

If you believe it's a good idea to leave your deer carcass hanging outside for an extended amount of time, this photo of a blowfly maggot from a deer carcass should give you ample reason to change your mind.

table, they begin cutting up the deer using the tools at hand. They do so despite the fact that the weather may be so frigid that they rush through their work, which usually leads to a lot of wasted meat. Most times, butchering deer in this manner ends with the hunters not being able to do the job as thoroughly as it would have been done indoors. Moreover, the entire process is seldom completed properly, nor is it performed under the best of sanitary conditions. Remember the flies.

Meat that is butchered outside is also subject to varying temperatures, dust, and dirt. More important, as I mentioned, it is often infested by hordes of flying insects including wasps, mosquitos, filthy houseflies, and nasty blowflies, all of which not only lay eggs in the meat, but will lick it, vomit, and defecate on it.

The DIY Butcher

The third group is the DIY faction. This group is growing by leaps and bounds. Each year, more and more hunters make the decision to home butcher their deer. There is no doubt this faction will soon be the largest of the four groups of hunters who home butcher game.

As I stated earlier, DIY butchers do so for a variety of reasons, including but not limited to: increasing the meat yield, eliminating the factor of not getting their own meat back, more efficient removal of deer hair, and being able to custom cut their meat. In other words, they opt to have total control of the butchering process of their deer.

Photo credit: Mike Ring.

These guys are hardcore DIY home butchers. Missing in the photo is Mike Ring, a fanatical deer hunter and DIY butcher too.

This particular group takes home butchering to a substantially higher level than the previous two groups. Statistically, they invest in buying a greater variety of quality tools and equipment. Some purchase or build sheds and/or erect tents to butcher their deer. Others build or convert home indoor working areas (home basements, an enclosed room in a garage, etc.), and understand the importance of having total control of butchering their venison, as well as breaking it down in a comfortable area under much more sanitary conditions.

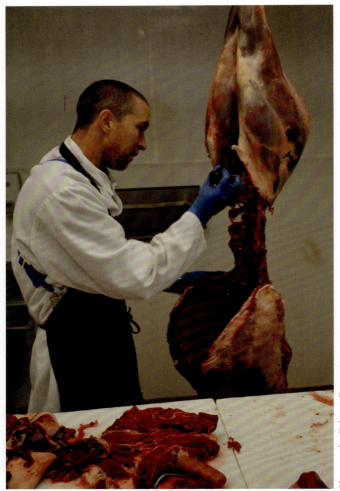

Photo credit: Fiduccia Enterprises.

Butchering deer indoors allows DIYers to take full control of the cleanliness and space they work in.

Professional Meat Cutters

The fourth group of hunters consists of professional meat cutters. They hold down full-time jobs as butchers of beef steers, cows, hogs, calves, lambs, and even poultry. Unlike the other three groups, this segment wants everything about their home butchering of deer to be as professional as when they butcher domestic animals at work. Like any professionals, they want to complete the job perfectly. To accomplish that goal, they must have every professionally made tool and piece of equipment possible. While we salute their aspiration of perfection, in reality an overwhelming number of hunters don't get involved to this degree with their DIY home butchering.

Photo credit: Game Butchers.

Like most professional butchers, JB Person is a stickler when it comes to processing deer meat. His processing plant includes a plethora of the latest butchering equipment available.

Therefore, while this book can be helpful to anyone who home butchers deer, it is more specifically *focused* on benefiting hunters who want to be able to complete the entire process safely, properly, safely, sanitarily, safely, comfortably, safely, out of the elements, while acquiring skills to elevate their home butchering techniques to the next level for years to come. Note the repeated use of the word "safely." When using razor-sharp knives, saws (handheld and electronic), cleavers, and so on, it is not out of the question that a serious accident may occur. If home butchers don't constantly keep safety uppermost in their mind, an accident is bound to take place. This can be as serious as slicing or puncturing an artery or vein, or cutting off a finger. The importance of safety must never be ignored.

In summary, the most important elements of successful home butchering are: the right butchering tools and other butchering equipment, a clean and comfortable work area, and solid how-to butchering information. All

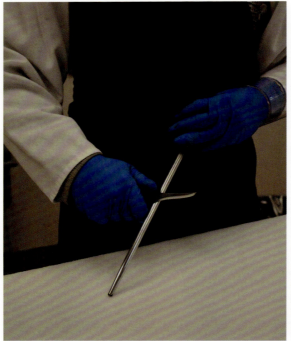

Photo credit: Fiduccia Enterprises.

When it comes to DIY butchering at home, the subject of safety must remain the #1 priority. Part and parcel of good safety procedures when using knives and other cutting tools is to keep them razor-sharp.

of these will make the undertaking much more enjoyable and it will make the time you cut up each deer go more quickly, easily, and trouble-free.

Before you decide to butcher your next deer, first remember that it requires an investment not only of time, but also of money. How much you actually spend will depend on just how well-equipped you want your home butcher shop to be outfitted. I do recommend starting off slowly when buying butchering tools, however. Once you have discovered you like butchering your own deer, then you can expand the line of tools as well as the type of indoor area used for butchering.

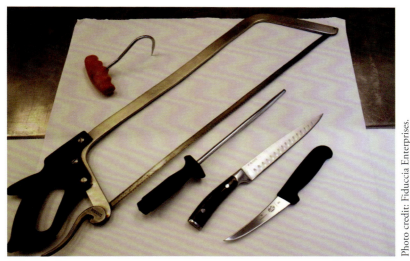

Photo credit: Fiduccia Enterprises.

Until a DIYer decides butchering deer at home is something he wants to expand on, he should start out with the minimal number of tools, shown in the photo above.

Chapter 11

Tools of the Trade

The majority of DIY hunters who cut up their deer or other big game no doubt do so not out of necessity, but by choice. Most do so because they either heard of or have had one or more bad experiences with a commercial meat-processing facility processing their deer. Some of the complications encountered can include: the high cost, loss of meat, long waiting times, less than clean facilities, inadequate packaging and/or labeling, and most important, not knowing if the meat you are getting back is actually from *your* own deer.

Meat lugs (tubs) are an important tool for the DIYer. They keep meat cool and neatly sorted, and are easy to clean. They are available in many of the sporting goods big-box stores, including Cabela's and Bass Pro Shops.

For these reasons, as well as a deep desire to butcher what they kill, a lot of hunters decide to butcher their deer or other big-game animals. There are many benefits tied to butchering your own game, including the gratification of learning how to do it correctly. After all, butchering the meat you have hunted is an important part of the entire hunt and it enhances the whole experience. Another important element is that most folks enjoy the fact that they have total control of the entire butchering process. Knowing that you can properly carry out all aspects of the hunt, from field to table, is extremely satisfying to hunters as well, as most DIY projects are.

Another aspect to learning all hunting skills (accurate one-shot kills, field dressing, skinning, quartering, butchering, aging, and cooking) is that there is no throwing away of mistakes. A piece of meat cut incorrectly simply ends up in another pile, to be ground into burger. Just remember this one important point: Anyone can properly learn the DIY aspects to butchering a deer or other big-game animal at home. The skills are not hard to acquire, and with each passing year a hunter's abilities will get better and better.

With all of that said, however, the most important elements of successful butchering at home are having the right tools, equipment, and work area to make the task go quickly, easily, and enjoyably. As with any DIY project, the right tools assure a more professional result. Therefore, before you decide to butcher your next deer, first remember that it requires an investment not only of time, but also of money. How much money will depend on just how well equipped a person wants to be. The good thing about home butchering is, however, that it can also be done on a limited budget, with a simple set of tools.

The fact is that a deer can be butchered with nothing more than a set of quality tools, including a hunting knife, saw, and knife sharpener. Deer hunters have used these tools to successfully butcher deer for countless years. But that doesn't mean that these tools are the best tools to use most effectively for the job at hand. Yes, there is something to be said for keeping the tools for butchering simple, but if you plan on butchering your own game on a long-term basis, your collection of tools should be more versatile. The old adage "use the right tools for the job" certainly applies to butchering game. This is particularly true because there is a significant safety factor to consider when using knives, hand saws, cleavers, hooks, and band saws. The wise home butcher, like the experienced carpenter, has a selection of versatile, high-quality tools.

Photo credit: Fiduccia Enterprises.

This basic set of tools will take care of everything from field dressing to skinning and butchering.

Some home butchers think that all the tools they need are just cutting and sharpening devices. When it comes to butchering deer, some tools are necessary to have at your disposal and some are not, even though they are handy to have. But, depending on how involved the home butcher wants to become, the optional tools are nice to have too.

Photo credit: Browning.

As your butchering skills develop, your desire to add more tools will too. This kit allows for more cutting and sharpening options, both in the field and at the butchering table.

When purchasing tools, particularly the cutting tools, select the best blades you can afford to buy. For instance, a high-quality hunting knife can be one of the most important and best investments a hunter can make. Like any tool, when it is selected correctly, used properly, and well taken care of, it will last a lifetime. This is not the case for any inexpensive knife or other butchering tools.

When buying quality butchering knives (saws, cleavers, or any tools with blades), look carefully at the materials used to make them. First and foremost, the steel of the blades of your knives should be stainless. They should be sturdy (hard) but not frail. A blade's Rockwell (the hardness rating given to a blade) should be about 58 to 60 in order for it to retain its edge. However, the blade must also be soft enough to allow for easy re-sharpening when it eventually becomes dull. It should be noted here that a knife blade used only for field dressing doesn't have to be long. In fact, a blade that is three and one-half to four and one-half inches long is more than sufficient for eviscerating a deer or most other big game.

Photo credit: Fiduccia Enterprises.

When purchasing knives, don't be a skinflint (cheap). Quality materials that make a top-notch knife blade will always be costlier than cheaply made blades. Research the materials used to make your knives and other cutting tools.

Another element that is often overlooked is the handle. This is an important component to be aware of. Handles should be constructed of hard materials such as wood, plastic, or a rugged synthetic, all of which will last much longer than other materials.

Still another factor to consider before buying a knife or other handheld cutting tool is comfort. Does the handle feel comfortable in your hand? A well-fitting knife will fit securely in your hands and is going to perform much better than one that doesn't fit well. An uncomfortable knife will also cause strain to the hand and wrist after you have used it for a while.

There are a wide variety of different types of points on knife blades (especially field-dressing knives) to choose from. They include drop points, gut hooks, and clip hooks. A clip-point blade is designed for more precise cutting. It will do the best job in opening the abdominal membrane when field dressing a deer or other big-game animal. Because the tip of the blade is curved upward higher than other blade tips, it will be less likely to rupture the intestines when slicing open the abdominal skin. It is wise to do your homework before selecting the type of knife tip you want, particularly on your field-dressing hunting knife.

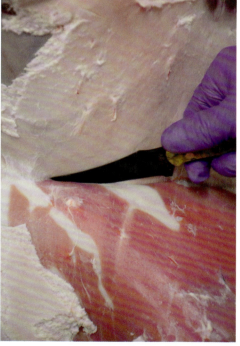

Photo credit: P. Cody Fiduccia.

Additionally, there is a large selection of hunting knife blades from which to choose. Some hunters prefer a fixed blade carried in a quality leather sheath. Others like the convenience of a folding blade because it is generally lighter to carry. A folder also offers a safety factor in that the blade isn't exposed. In fact, all folding knife blades

When making precise cuts, a small slip hook blade will perform well. Different points on knife blades are designed to serve different functions. The more a DIYer gets involved in butchering, the greater his selection of knife points.

should have a feature that locks them into place once the blade is opened. The blade should remain rigidly in place while in use. When buying any type of field-dressing and/or butchering knives or other cutting implements, it is also crucial to remember that a sharp, quality blade will not only consistently perform better when cutting, it will also provide the hunter/DIY butcher more control when cutting and, therefore, is safer to use. There is absolutely no doubt that all your hunting knives and other cutting blades should be as

Photo credit: Fiduccia Enterprises.

Some hunters prefer to use folding blades to field dress a deer, as they are compact and light to carry. As a safety factor, use only folding knives that lock in place.

sharp as a Klingon's *d'k tahg or bat'leth* (you thought I wouldn't get another *Star Trek* reference in this book, didn't you?).

Some of the same types of features found on hunting knives are present on butchering knives. When shopping for butchering knives, consider that they will come in every conceivable design. This can make your decision about which knives to purchase a bit confusing. To butcher a deer effectively, though, an assortment of knives (and other cutting tools) will be most useful, as each has been developed to perform a specific task. When cutting up a deer, for example, it is best to have a knife at the ready expressly designed for a certain cut, as opposed to wishing that you had one. You don't want to end up having to use a substitute knife to make the cut instead. Remember, like a plumber, carpenter, or any other contractor, the proper tools make the user perform the best job possible.

As a graduate of Cornell University's Hotel School, an author of several wild game cookbooks, an experienced big-game hunter, and the director of New York Custom Processing (a beef processing plant), my wife, Kate, has a large selection of chef knives, including a complete

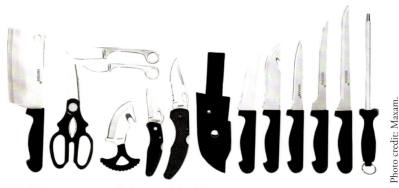

This fifteen-piece set includes everything but a meat saw, which can be purchased separately anyway. It provides a wide array of field-dressing and butchering tools for the home butcher. This kit is available at www.deerdoctor. com at a special discount price.

set of butchering blades that she keeps in a special case. Not every DIY home butcher who cuts up his own deer and other game needs such an inclusive choice of blades, however. If the truth be told, the bulk of home butchers can get by rather nicely with no more than a half dozen *quality* cutting tools. Most DIY butchers find, though, that the longer they butcher their own deer, the more they want a wider selection of knives rather than the standard complement of four to six knives. This decision is usually a wise one.

The cutting tools are meant to cut the meat off the bones, slice steaks, cut roasts, dice up stew meat, butterfly cutlets, slice medallions, cut up meat portions to be made into burger, trim the tallow, cut away silverskin, and cut up all the disposable leftover inedible meat (bloodshot, etc.). The one important feature to look for in all handheld knives, cleavers, and saws is a full tang. A knife that has a full-tang blade is one where the metal of the blade goes all the way through the handle. It should also have strong rivets to hold the handle securely to the blade. Full-tang knives are sturdier and therefore easier to work with.

Following is a rundown of all the type of knives, other cutting instruments, and accessories that can be used in the field dressing and butchering process. The more of these that you have, the better equipped you will be to do a first-rate job.

Knives

Photo credit: Fiduccia Enterprises.

Conventional Butcher Knife: A selection of butchering knives should include a traditional knife with a blade that is eight to twelve inches long. This knife is mostly used to slice large pieces of meat into smaller portions. The size of the blade enables the user to cut these chunks cleanly with one single cut. A shorter blade would take several cuts to complete the same task. This knife is also known as a carver or slicer blade. A Japanese Santoku knife is but one example of this type of knife blade, which is designed to slice, dice, or mince.

Curved Butcher Knife: A ten-inch curved butcher knife is the utilitarian knife in a DIY butcher's knife collection. If a lot of steak cutting will be done from the loin, short loin, sirloin, or round, the DIYer may want to consider purchasing a curved butchering knife. The blade allows for long, deep cuts in a single draw. To make a professional looking steak cut, a ten-inch curved butcher's knife is nice to have.

Boning Knife: This is the one knife no butcher can do without. It is a crucial piece of butchering equipment and can have a blade that is curved or straight. If curved, the blade can be flexible or stiff. It is usually four to eight inches long, though most butchers prefer a length of six inches. While the curved and flexible blade is primarily used to remove meat from the bone, the straight boning knives are generally used for separating joints and cutting tendons found at the ends of muscles. To bone out meat quickly, easily, and safely, this knife is a must-have item. By boning out deer meat with a boning knife instead of using a hand saw (or an electric band saw), you will prevent tiny pieces of marrow, bone, and cartilage from getting on the meat that is being cut. The fact is, marrow is second only to tallow (deer fat) for making delicious deer meat taste objectionably pungent (gamey). It should be noted that boning out deer meat is a very good idea instead of leaving the meat with "bone in." This is particularly true if you are short on freezer space. Boned-out meat will take up much less room in the freezer than meat left on the bone. I prefer a boning knife to any other knife, including the more expensive custom butchering hunting knives. As butchering knives go, a boning knife is inexpensive. The blade is also soft enough to sharpen in a hurry.

Fillet Knife: While a boning knife can also be used as a fillet knife, there are differences between the two. Most novice DIY butchers confuse them. Generally speaking, a boning knife is self-explanatory—it is meant to remove meat from bones. A fillet knife has a long, thin, flat, flexible blade. It is commonly used for removing bones and skin from meat. The flexibility

Photo credit: www.deerdummy.com

A boning knife is a must-have cutting tool for anyone who butchers deer or other meat. It is invaluable when separating tendons, boning meat, and trimming. It is probably the most versatile knife blade used for butchering. This blade is available from www.deerdummy.com.

and thinness offered in a true fillet knife helps the user to perform the more precise cuts that are required for more delicate meats such as butterflying the medallions of the backstrap. The fillet knife blade sometimes curves up while the boning knife is generally straight. The reason for the confusion between a true boning and a

As with any knife, there is a myriad of shapes and sizes to each blade. This is one option for a butchering fillet knife.

fillet knife is that there is some overlap in use between the two. Boning knives can be used for filleting, and there are some all-purpose bone/fillet knives. In the end, the novice DIY butcher can get by with just a boning knife. As your hobby develops, however, and more tools are added, and butchering experience is gained, the DIY butcher will most likely want to add a true fillet knife to his or her collection of cutting tools.

Skinning Knife: The blade of a quality skinning knife should be about five to six inches in length. The rounded curve is specially designed to cleanly slice away the hide from the skin of the deer. The curvature allows for longer cuts with each draw of the blade. The blunted point is particularly helpful to reduce accidental punctures of the hide. When using a quality skinning knife, and when the job is done properly with a

Here are a few different types of blades—both in size and shape—that will serve to skin a deer. There are many other options from which to choose. It's important to buy one that fits comfortably in your hand.

sharp knife, very little force has to be applied to separate the hide from the deer carcass.

Heavy Cleaver: First and foremost, a quality meat cleaver should have a stainless-steel blade strong enough to withstand chopping bone, cartilage, and so on. It should also offer the user versatility (i.e., chopping through a leg bone or slicing a large piece of meat). When buying a cleaver, it is important to make sure the handle is sturdy, comfortable, and *non-slip*. It must also have a full tang with strong rivets, where the blade runs through the entire handle. Any knife or cleaver that is fully tanged will last a long time. It also offers an important element of safety when using a cleaver for chopping. A cleaver should also be well-balanced to prevent it from slipping out of your hand, and also to prevent your wrist from tiring during use.

The blunt back edge of a cleaver can also be used to tenderize meat. High-quality materials found in more expensive cleavers include high-carbon German steel, which is rust-resistant, strong, and holds an edge longer.

Photo credit: Maxam.

No assortment of butchering tools is complete without a quality cleaver. While it's important your knives have full-tang blades, it is critical that a cleaver has one.

Saws

Sturdy Handsaw (Meat Saw): A meat handsaw is constructed just like a hacksaw, with a thin blade that is tensioned. Generally, they come in blade lengths of seventeen to thirty inches. A hand saw that is twenty-five to thirty inches long will provide the widest range of use. Blades are available with several options for the number of teeth per inch, with a general-purpose blade having ten teeth per inch. They are used for separating the shoulder from the loin, splitting the shoulder into the chuck and shank

Photo credit: www.webrestaurantstore.com

Many home butchers make a mistake by buying meat saws that don't do the job well. The old adage, "You get what you pay for," applies here. Buy a quality saw with the right number of teeth in its blade and a sturdy handle, and it will make a world of difference in your home butchering.

halves, splitting the loin from the sirloin, sawing off leg parts, and cutting the carcass in half.

Electric Table Band Saw (optional)

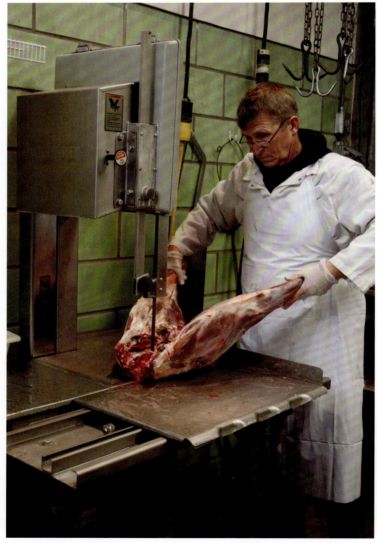

Photo credit: GameButchers.

An electric band saw makes short work of cutting through bones. However, they're expensive and can be dangerous and are generally only used by home butchers who have decades of experience.

Sharpening Devices

Photo credit: Fiduccia Enterprises.

- Coarse and fine stone handheld sharpener
- Electric sharpener (Chef's Choice)
- Sharpening steel (small one for the field, larger one for processing)
- Whet stone

Hoisting Equipment

- Block and tackle
- Come-along

Electrical Equipment

- Meat grinder (electric with feeding pan and meat plunger)
- Meat slicer
- Vacuum sealer (with different sizes of vacuum pouches)

Photo credit: Fiduccia Enterprises.

Other Items

- Apron
- Arm guard
- Cavity spreader, stainless steel (Outdoor Edge brand)
- Cleaning solutions (bleach/water or vinegar/water)
- Cutting boards (white poly plastic)

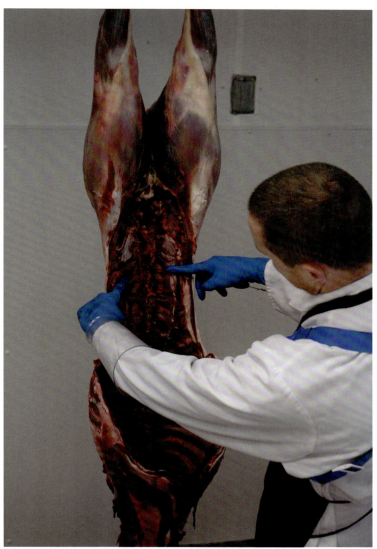

Photo credit: Fiduccia Enterprises.

- Food services gloves
- Freezer paper and tape
- Gambrel with curved arms or ends
- Game bags
- Kitchen scale
- Kitchen string (for tying roasts)
- Marking pen
- Meat bins (or large plastic bowls)
- Meat pole with stainless steel hooks (that don't rust)
- Meat tenderizer (Jaccard).
- Rags/paper towels
- Ropes
- Rubber food service gloves
- Sausage casings (optional)
- Sausage stuffer (optional)
- Water (running water, hose, buckets of water)
- Stainless-steel cavity spreader (Outdoor Edge)

Safety Equipment: The safety equipment noted here is highly recommended, whether this is the first deer you are butchering or the fiftieth. As an FYI, in case you have become overly confident or nonchalant because you have used and handled knives and other cutting tools for a long time, all the professional butchers at my wife Kate's beef-processing plant are required to have safety items while cutting meat. Keep this fact in mind when using butchering tools. It isn't a matter of *if* you are going to cut yourself, it's a matter of *when* you will cut yourself. Regularly using safety equipment can significantly reduce the severity of knife injuries. All safety protection devices are found on the web. Be cautious when doing your research to purchase them. Make sure the company you deal with is reputable.

Knife scabbard. A scabbard provides a safe place for you to put your knives when they are not in use, and also keeps them readily handy. A scabbard made of plastic is safer and less expensive than one made of leather or some other type of material. As mentioned above, all commercial meat plants require the meat cutters to wear scabbards or have them attached to the side of their meat boning tables. They are required to do this in order to help prevent injuries. Leaving knives lying about on tables and such will always end up leading to butchers getting accidental cuts. Some are minor and others can be literally life threatening.

Photo credit: Fiduccia Enterprises.

Boning glove(s). A boning glove is either made of stainless steel mesh or Kevlar. It is designed to prevent cuts to the hand that is NOT holding the knife by slicing or stabbing. Most accidental cuts do indeed happen to the hand not using the knife. The Kevlar gloves are more prone to allowing a knife to stab through them. Knowing that, most professional butchers refrain from sharpening the tips of their knives to a stiletto point.

Knife hand glove. This is the same as the Kevlar boning glove above but it is thinner in order to

Photo credit: Fiduccia Enterprises.

Home butchering accidents mostly occur to fingers. If you would like to keep all your digits intact, a metal mesh glove is a good investment.

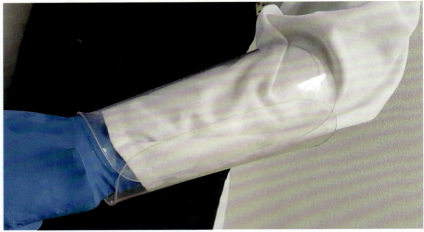

This wrist/arm guard can save a DIY butcher from serious injury and even death. It should be worn every time meat is butchered.

allow for better grip and use of the knife hand. This glove helps to prevent stabbing injuries.

Wrist guard. A wrist guard is worn over the wrist, above the boning glove. These guards come in Kevlar and what is referred to as tube plastic wrist guards. While most professional butchers say the Kevlar version is more comfortable to wear, they also say that the Kevlar is less effective in preventing stab wounds.

Belly Guard. For guys like me, whose belly wants to get in the way when butchering deer, this piece of equipment is even more important than it is for those whose bellies aren't as suicidal. A belly guard is a "cut and stab proof" guard worn around the waist and fastened to a special belt. Most chain types are very expensive and difficult to find. The ones made of "cut-proof"

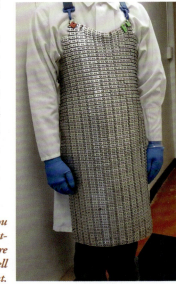

You may think a metal apron is overdoing it, but you would be wrong. The more deer you butcher, the greater the chance of an injury occurring. While they are expensive (ranging from $100 to $200), they are well worth the money to help prevent a serious accident.

plastic are just as effective and cost less. Most professional butchers say they are more comfortable to wear. (*This is a crucial piece of safety equipment. No one should leave to chance the possibility of puncturing their femoral artery.*) While most manufacturers of belly guards say they are cut proof, I tend to believe it is better to be safe than sorry. Like a wrist watch that's sold as being "waterproof," I am leery about any manufacturer's claim that a belly guard is completely "cut and stab proof."

Sharpening Tips

No matter how defined your selection of tools is, the most important element is how effectively you use them. The most basic of all facts about butchering is that you cannot butcher meat properly without a selection of sharp knives and other cutting tools. I have my own saying (in fact I have several) about using sharp cutting tools. *"A butcher without a sharp knife ends up truly being 'a butcher' in the worse sense of the word."* Equally important is also making sure that all the other cutting tools, saw blades, and grinder knives (blades)/ plates, and anything else used to cut with always have sharp edges. While some people are adept at using sharpening stones and steels manually, not everyone is, and some simply can't ever learn to use them properly.

When I worked at Tomaso's Butcher shop, the owner, Louie, had a saying: *"You can't keep a sharp edge on a knife without using a honing-steel."* A quality sharpening steel is probably one of the most misunderstood and misused pieces of butchering equipment. While there is no doubt Louie was correct, there is a learning curve attached to how to properly and effectively use a sharpening steel. In addition, there are a variety of honing steels to do different things. They include flat, round, medium, fine, coarse, diamond, ceramic, and so on, and are made in varying lengths. Any worthwhile butcher will tell you that a quality sharpening steel is among the most necessary tools he/she

Photo credit: Fiduccia Enterprises.

Steels come in a wide variety of shapes (round, flat, etc.), surfaces (fine, rough, etc.), and compositions (diamond, steel, ceramic, etc.). Having more than one type of steel allows you to keep an edge on any of your butchering knives.

uses. They will also agree that it is worthwhile for DIY butchers to learn how to use one properly.

Remember this about properly using a honing steel: It has been my experience, with every professional butcher I have ever met, that they touch a knife's blade to a sharpening steel with a full stroke so delicately that the resulting noise from the contact being made between knife blade and sharpening steel is barely audible. I sometimes have to bite my lip (or giggle) when I see someone slashing a knife blade across a sharpening steel so hard and fast that it is enough to make sparks fly. They must be confusing a sharpening steel for a fire-starter!

Seriously, though, they make contact so fast and so hard that it's easy to hear the contact being made from two rooms away. Under these circumstances, the message these people send to others is *"I'm a total amateur at using a sharpening steel to hone a knife edge."*

In the end, after you have used a sharpening steel many times and still can't get it to sharpen your blades, you may be among those who simply find it impractical to learn how to use a honing steel correctly. Worry not, though, as there is a much less frustrating alternative. To make the job easier and ensure a razor-sharp edge, the option is to use an electric knife sharpener that comes with various stones for different levels of sharpening. One company that offers a wide line of all types of electric and handheld sharpeners (one handheld unit specially designed for hunters and anglers is called the Sportsman), as well as sharpening files, diamond hones and stones, and diamond sharpening steels is Chef's Choice by EdgeCraft (www.chefschoice .com).

Finally, when it comes to tools, the adage "Cleanliness is next to godliness" couldn't be more accurate. Keeping all your butchering

Photo credit: Fiduccia Enterprises.

The old saying "Take care of your tools and they will take care of you" applies to your butchering tools. Keep them sharp and clean, and they'll always function at peak performance.

tools not only sharp, and in tip-top condition, but thoroughly sparkling clean is paramount to good tasting, flavorful meat free from being tainted by dirty equipment. If there was ever a time to be fussy about cleanliness, keeping your tools and work area spotless, it is during the process of butchering the meat.

One last word of warning: With all the hoopla about TSEs (transmissible spongiform encephalopathies) and CWD (chronic wasting disease), it is wise to steer clear of touching or cutting any brain or spinal tissue or fluid. This is why it is crucial that you make sure you use surgical gloves. They should be worn during the entire process of butchering your deer. Additionally, the gloves you wear protect the meat you are cutting from whatever contaminants may be on your hands.

Butchering Kit

As a special offer to those who purchase this book, you can buy our ten-piece Game Processing Set (with a mfg. lifetime warranty) at a special price. The set includes full-tang stainless-steel blades, so you'll never find yourself in a bind when it's time to process your deer or other big game. The triple-rivet Leymar handles are specifically designed to offer a comfortable, safe grip. The kit includes a meat saw with three extra stainless-steel saw blades, a sharpening steel, 13½-inch meat cleaver, 11½-inch butcher knife, 9½-inch field-dressing knife with gut hook, 8¼-inch skinning/caping knife, and a 7-inch all-purpose knife to trim meat off bones, fat, and other general use. The kit also includes a 10-inch utilitarian pair of shears. The kit comes packaged in a blow-molded case and comes with a manufacturer's limited lifetime warranty. This set regularly retails for $57.95. But, for a limited time, it is being offered at more than a 20 percent discount for only $46. Visit our website at deerdoctor. com for more detailed information.

Photo credit: Fiduccia Enterprises.

Chapter 12

Butchering Your Deer

The first time a person butchers a deer, the hanging carcass can be intimidating. One can easily feel as if he or she took on a project that is more than they can handle. The reality, however, is that breaking down an entire deer into quarter pieces and then into smaller cuts isn't all that difficult or troublesome. I want to emphasize that point by assuring readers, particularly those who have never butchered their own deer, that cutting up a deer into portions is nothing to be anxious about, it's simply not that *big* of a deal. It only appears that way at first.

The anxiety is usually caused because the size of the deer compels the would-be butcher into a false belief that the deer is larger than it actually is. An adult *field-dressed* male deer averages 120 to 130 pounds (some adult males are usually heavier) and stands about thirty-nine inches at the shoulder. That's not

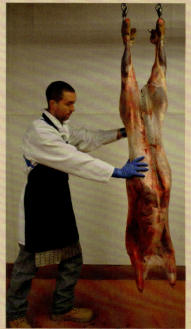

A hanging deer carcass can be intimidating to many first-time DIY home butchers, so much so that they don't know where to start. The fact is, the learning curve is rather short, the process is straightforward, and with a little practice you'll be a pro in no time.

all that large, especially when compared to a hanging carcass of a 1,200-pound plus steer, a 1,000 pound moose, or a 700-pound elk.

Breaking Down the Carcass

Another worrisome and perplexing issue is that many hunters who butcher their first deer start with a mindset that erroneously compares the task of breaking down a deer to the butchering of a steer. They'll wonder, "How do I cut that thing into T-bone steaks, prime ribs, filet mignon, short ribs, New York strips, boned ribs, rump roasts, sirloin steaks, bottom and top rounds, and so on?" It is understandable how frustrating, confusing, and sometimes even upsetting that can be, especially for a beginner.

The fact of the matter is that a steer is so large that it produces much more meat and requires a lot more butchering work. Each cut is given a special name to make it sound more appetizing and appealing when it is marketed in the store showcase. Conversely, a deer simply breaks down into many smaller amounts of the same cuts a steer produces but with not as much fancy terminology. A New York strip steak cut from a deer is simply termed a venison steak.

A deer carcass produces three basic steaks: tenderloin, sirloin, and round steak. That's pretty straightforward, yes? Even more surprising to someone new to butchering their own deer is that there are only three

Photo credit: Fiduccia Enterprises.

Unlike the myriad of general cuts of meat, as well as highly specialized cuts made to a beef carcass, a deer carcass breaks down to smaller cuts, and a lot fewer specialized cuts.

kinds of roasts: one from each rear leg, called the rump roast; one from each shoulder, called the shoulder roast; and one from the neck (yup, neck roast). The rest of the meat from the deer is used mostly as ground meat, stew meat, sausages, or for small chunks in chili. That's all there is to it.

If you haven't already broken the deer down to quarters, this will be the first step in butchering your hanging carcass. As described in the chapter about how to quarter your deer, breaking down your deer into four convenient pieces is almost identical to how a steer carcass is quartered (two forequarters and two hindquarters). However, at this point, when you begin butchering, you will have two fore legs, two hind legs, two tenderloins, two backstraps, and a carcass with neck and ribs.

The Ups and Downs

Although a deer can be quartered and broken down by hanging from either its head or hind legs, it's really a matter of personal choice as to how you hang it. It should also be noted, though, that each hanging position makes the steps of breaking the deer down *somewhat* different. After a little experience, you will find which position works best for you. Most professional butchers, hunters, and DIY home butchers find it a lot easier to skin, quarter, and break a deer down when the deer is hanging by rear legs (head down).

I also find it most comfortable to work on a deer when it is hung through the tough rear leg tendons, which hold it securely and safely while I am working with knives and other

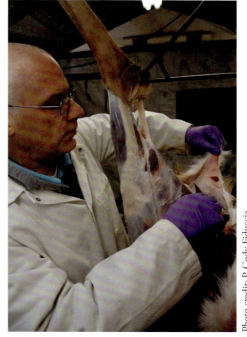

Photo credit: P. Cody Fiduccia.

Most DIY butchers hang deer by the rear legs by placing a steel hook or stout gambrel through the rear tendons, which helps the carcass hang more securely. It also makes for easier removal of the hide and breaking down the carcass into quarters.

cutting tools. For me, when the carcass is hung by the rear legs, it is easier to separate the quarters, particularly the front leg/shoulder from the carcass in this position. This is principally the case because there is no ball-and-socket in the front leg/shoulder as found in the rear legs.

To Bone In or to Bone Out

Before making the first cut, a decision has to be made about how the entire carcass will be butchered. There are two options: bone in or bone out. Each is said to have its own benefits depending on the meat cuts preferred, and equally important, the tools that will be used to butcher the carcass.

As the term itself describes, the bone in method simply means some portions of the carcass will be cut through the bones and other cuts will be butchered with the meat purposely left on bones. While the bone in method provides more traditional cuts (loin chops, ribs, short ribs, and other cuts with the bone left in), this method ends up being a lot more work. It also takes a greater amount of butchering time and requires additional tools, some of which are considerably more expensive than tools needed for boning out a carcass.

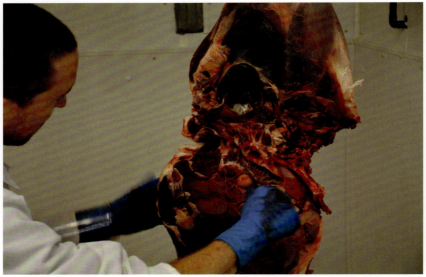

Photo credit: Fiduccia Enterprises.

Boning out the meat of an entire carcass makes the task of butchering the deer go quicker and easier. It also provides more meat.

When butchering deer with the bone in method, there are a host of important caveats to be considered. Bone in butchering can end up tainting the meat with bone chips, fat, sinew, tallow, and, worst of all, marrow. The marrow can seep out of the bones during cooking, making your meal considerably less palatable than it could be.

Another negative reason against using the bone in method is related to Chronic Wasting Disease (CWD). All CWD advisories suggest avoiding cutting through any of the bones and particularly cutting through the spinal column. (When you bone out meat, the first thing you do is split the spinal column—not a good choice if you are concerned about CWD).

That in itself is reason enough to abandon cutting up deer bone in, and instead using the boneless method. By doing so, it will decrease the chances of possibly contracting CWD.

With all that said about bones, however, there will still be some hunters who want to save the bones to make soup stocks despite the cautionary advisories about CWD (avoid fluids and other materials from bones). That's enough reason for me, and should be for you, not to use deer bones for soup stock. Another reason is Kate's reaction to the idea of saving deer bones for stock—"yuck." I agree. Dispose of them.

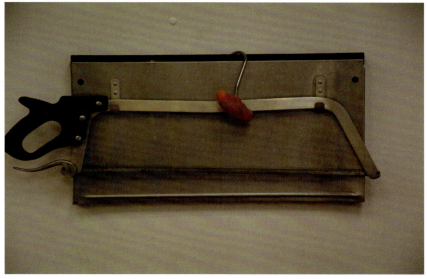

Photo credit: Fiduccia Enterprises.

When butchering a carcass the bone in way, use a high-quality hand saw as one of your tools. A high-end hand saw will also benefit the DIY butcher for all other butchering methods that require being cut using a saw.

If you're hell-bent on using the bone in method, however, it pays to use a high-quality, professional handsaw. They have about ten to twelve teeth per inch and the blade and saw will last for years. This will eliminate the headaches caused by using a less expensive saw. Cheaper blades for hand saws will have twice as many teeth that easily get clogged up with meat and bone and have to be cleaned constantly during the butchering process. Again, this is yet another negative reason not to use the bone in method. But if you prefer to butcher the carcass using the bone in technique, you should also invest in a new or used electric band saw. You can find an affordable used band saw at most restaurant and/or butcher supply houses.

Yet, another objection I have about breaking down a deer leaving the bones in, or "bone in," is that the fat and marrow from the bones can turn meat rancid when it is stored in the freezer. As mentioned in the storage chapter, boned-out meat is much easier to wrap and it also takes much less room to store in the freezer.

Bone Out

The bone out method simply means that the meat is cut away from all the bones. As I have repeatedly said (in order to drive my point home), the bone out technique is the easiest method to use to butcher a deer or other big-game animal. Many of the cuts from the bone in way are the same as those produced by the boning-out system, without the bother of dealing with the bones. With that said, though, many times the ribs are not used, particularly on a very small deer, when employing the bone out system. However, if you have the

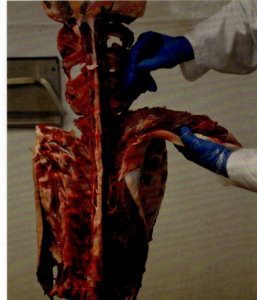

Photo credit: Fiduccia Enterprises.

The bone out method simply removes all meat from the bones.

time, the meat can be cut away from the ribs and used for trim to be put into ground/sausage meat.

When boning out a deer, the easy way to estimate the final boned-out amount of product you can expect to get is to divide the field-dressed weight of the deer in half. Or Google the National Research Institute and search "Estimating Deer Weight from Field-Dressed Weight." There you will discover several helpful charts on this subject. Keep in mind that the total bone out ratio will change depending upon how much meat has been damaged by the projectile used. It will also change depending upon whether or not the animal has been hung in proper conditions before being broken down.

Boneless butchering is much easier than bone in butchering. The process is so straight-forward it can even be done blindfolded—but don't try this at home, kids. Additionally, many professional butchers and chefs state that boning out venison most often results in tastier meat.

Once the deer has been broken down as described in chapter 6, "A Step-by-Step Manual to Quartering," you will end up with the two tenderloins. Once the carcass is cooled, the tenderloins are very easy to simply pull free of the carcass. They should be removed first from the inside of the rib cage. It should be noted that the quartering chapter mentions how to remove the backstraps. Removing the backstraps can also be done prior to quartering the deer. If you choose to do that, there is nothing wrong about it. In fact, many hunters remove the backstraps soon after the deer is hung.

Photo credit: Fiduccia Enterprises.

To end up with better tasting meat, follow the advice of many professional chefs and butchers, by boning out your carcass.

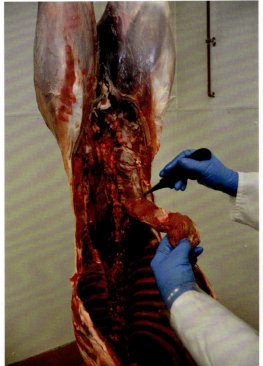

Photo credit: Fiduccia Enterprises.

Here, a single tenderloin is being removed by guiding the knife along the bone to free the meat. The tender- loins can also be gently pulled free of the ribcage.

Remember that an important element to easier butchering is keeping the quarters as cool as possible. While working on one quarter, the other quarters should be kept in a refrigerator or other cool area like a garage or shed, as long as you take the time to cover each piece in a game bag. To further reduce the chances of bacterial growth on the meat you're boning, as you are cutting the various portions, it is wise to bone and refrigerate each cut until you are ready to pack and freeze.

Fat, Silverskin, and Tendons

Start the boning process with a very important element about achieving tastier venison. Despite the fact that most hunters have been told that all fat is termed as "tallow," that is not the case. Actually, there are three different types of fat. The tallow fat we are all familiar with is located mostly on the back of the deer and it mainly covers the rump section, with a little of it also found on the neck and the front shoulder.

The next nomenclature for fat is referred to as cod fat. This is located only on the brisket. The last type of fat terminology is denoted as marbling. Yes, deer do have (fat) marbling, something I was genuinely surprised to discover as a younger hunter. I had always heard and/or read, probably like most of you have, that deer meat has no marbling, or at least not enough to speak of. Live and learn.

Cod and tallow fat are located on the external surfaces of the deer's anatomy, just under the deer's hide. For a majority of people who enjoy

Photo credit: P. Cody Fiduccia.

There are three different types of fat on deer. They are called tallow, cod, and marbling fat. The latter is rarely found within the meat of wild deer, especially when it is compared to domestic meats.

eating venison, these two fats have a distinct flavor. The older the deer is, the more noticeable the taste of cod and tallow fat becomes. For my taste buds, and probably most anyone who eats venison, the flavor of cod and tallow fat can be described as nothing short of *awful*.

Contrarily, marbling fat is said by many meat professionals to be the only worthwhile fat on a deer. It is found interlaced throughout the deer's muscle fibers. It appears like thin, stretched-out, long white lines or streaks. Again, meat authorities recommend that marbling fat should not be trimmed away during the butchering process. Research says that marbling fat in deer is essentially tasteless, although the research goes on to state that marbling fat does significantly enhance the tenderness (not necessarily the flavor) of cooked venison.

Another point I would like to make is that while butchering all the cuts made while processing your deer, you should take time to remove as much cod and tallow fat as possible. Don't get carried away spending an inordinate amount of time trimming fat, however. I know some DIY butchers who get totally mired down with removing every tiny piece of fat they see while butchering the deer. It's simply not necessary to get stalled removing *all* the silverskin and tiny pieces of fat from the meat while you are butchering it. Any small pieces that are left on the meat after the deer has been butchered and all the meat has been trimmed, can go through a final stage of trimming to a finer degree once the meat is defrosted (and still somewhat cool) and is being prepared to be cooked. By following these guidelines about trimming fat and silverskin, I assure you that your taste buds will appreciate your efforts.

Breaking Down the Front Leg/Shoulder

Breaking down the front leg (shoulder) from the main carcass is easier than removing the back leg from the carcass. This is because the front leg doesn't have a ball and socket, as is found in the back leg. The front leg only has a wide, flat bone called the scapula, which floats free of all the other bone connections within the deer's body. Only a few muscle segments attach the scapula to the body of the deer, which is why the entire front leg is easily removed with nothing more than a sharp knife. As most people who enjoy eating venison most likely know, the meat from the front shoulders doesn't provide the most tender cuts. This is particularly true when compared

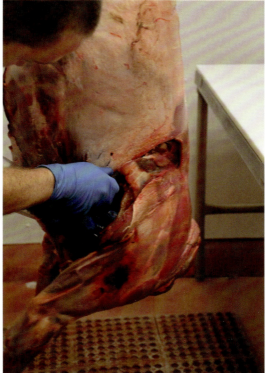

Photo credit: Fiduccia Enterprises.

The front legs are very easy to remove with just a sharp knife, as they don't have a ball and socket to cut through like back legs do.

to the meat found on the hindquarters, which is much more tender and flavorful.

Once you place the front leg and shoulder on your work area to be cut up, use a fillet knife and trim away the tallow fat, silverskin, and the thin protective layer of crust that the meat may have acquired while hanging on the meat pole.

Making Boneless Cuts from the Front Legs/Shoulders

The front leg/shoulder area includes the shoulder, arm, and shank. Since its meat isn't all that tender, it is mostly dedicated to making stew meat, pot roasts, and even jerky meat. Begin by breaking down the meat along the bony ridge found in the middle of the shoulder blade (scapula). One side will produce small pieces of boneless meat referred to as "chuck tender." This cut will be the best tender section of the shoulder. Then bone out the other side of the shoulder blade, which can be made into shoulder roasts.

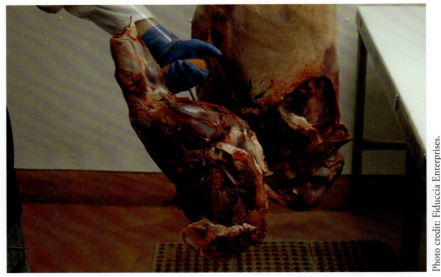

Photo credit: Fiduccia Enterprises.

Seen here are large amounts of cod and tallow fat as well as silverskin prior to it being trimmed away. Using a hand-hook tool to remove the heavy cuts will save you from a backache, and protect the meat from falling as well.

Next, trim away all the leftover meat on the shoulder blade. The combined cuts can be used to make shoulder and pot roasts. Grind the meat from the shank to use for burger. If you make jerky, use the chuck "tenders," which are also good to use for stew meat.

Removing the Hind Legs

Once a hind leg is lying on the cutting board, it will be made up of the sirloin tip, the bottom and top rounds, the eye round, a section of the rump, and, of course, the shank. The rump is the most popular cut on deer and other big game. The two tender cuts will be from the sirloins, rounds, and rumps. As anyone who has prepared and eaten venison knows, the meat

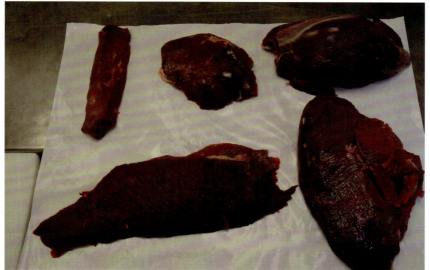

These cuts are considered prime cuts of a deer. Clockwise, from left to right, are the slender eye round, top butt, sirloin tip, top round, and bottom round.

Photo credit: Fiduccia Enterprises.

from the front leg/shoulder and hind leg shanks isn't as tender and, therefore, it is commonly reserved for use as ground meat and stew.

Once you have removed the silverskin that encases the hind leg, detach the top round from the remaining piece of the leg. There will be a natural layer where you can pull the top round away from the rest of the leg. If need be, use the tip of your knife to cut free any meat that doesn't pull away freely with your fingers. Now simply cut along the back of the leg and the top round will be freed from the rest of the leg.

With the leg facing away from you, now remove the sirloin tip. Your starting point will be at the top of the hard, white knuckle bone. Make a cut through the meat just above the knuckle at a slight angle. The knife blade will come into contact against the leg bone. At that point, turn the blade flat and bring the knife cut toward you, keeping the blade continually against the bone until the sirloin tip is cut totally free. (When cutting along the bones, the procedure is known by professional butchers as "following the bone.")

Once you have finished this cut, you have created a rectangle portion of solid, boneless meat called the sirloin tip. There are a few options to consider with this piece of meat. It can be left whole, and used as a sirloin tip roast, or it can be made into different size steaks. For instance, you can

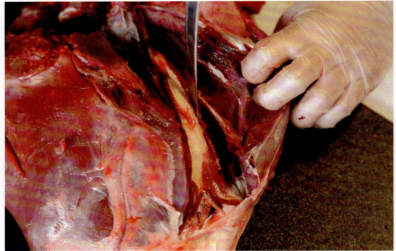

Photo credit: Kerry Swendsen, www.deerdummy.com

As seen here, cutting the sirloin tip begins at the top of the hard, white knuckle bone. While cutting, keep the knife blade continually against the bone. Kerry Swendsen, a meat-cutting professional, enhanced on the original motto "following the bone" and made his saying "follow-the-bone," famous.

vertically cut the meat into several tasty medium sirloin tip steaks, usually about three-quarters of an inch thick. They can also be used as Swiss steaks. The steaks in the middle of this piece of meat will usually be about the same size and thickness. But as you work toward the end, they will inevitably become smaller. The next step is the same, whether you want to use the rest of the rump for round steaks or for roasts.

Remove the entire bone without ruining any of the meat that envelops it. Using the tip of a sharp boning knife, cut slowly around edge while carefully pulling away the meat until you have reached the other side. By making two vertical slices, you will complete the separation at the lower leg and upper pelvic areas, freeing the meat in one large, boneless slab. (Working with cold meat during this process pays big dividends, as compared working with meat that is warm and therefore more difficult to control.) This large boneless portion can be sliced vertically into about four to six one-quarter to three-quarter-inch round steaks.

For those who enjoy eating larger steaks (width and length), make these steaks from the entire hind leg, which gives you yet another round steak possibility using the versatile and very popular rump meat. Instead of

Photo credit: Kerry Swendsen, www.deerdummy.com

When butchering deer meat, especially when trimming it from the bone, keep the carcass very cool. Cool temperatures will break down the carcass faster and make the butchering process go quicker and easier.

boning out the entire piece of rump as described above, make extra-large round steaks. Next cut across all the muscle groups rather than boning out the meat. Using a large butcher knife, slice down through the meat until your knife hits the bone (without damaging the bone), cutting large, thick individual steaks as you do this. Next, switch to a sharp fillet knife and carefully trim the meat around the leg bone. Then glide the newly cut steak portion over the knuckle of the leg bone. You can continue to make these extra-large steaks until you reach the shank portion of the hind leg. This technique ends up making steaks that will be the same size and shape and each of them will still end up not containing any bone or bone matter. The big steaks you just made can be one inch thick or more if you prefer.

If you enjoy roasts more than you do steaks, by all means make them from the rump instead of steaks. The roasts will be as tender and flavorful as any steak will be. The hind leg rump not only offers tender meat, it also offers a lot of options. The fact of the matter is that when cutting up the meat of the rump, you will end up with a lot of large, medium, and smaller portions of steaks or roasts. If you feel up to it, consider butchering one hind as described above, and cut up the second rear leg slightly differently, into rolled rump roasts and so on.

Photo credit: Kerry Swendsen, www.deerdummy.com

Different people enjoy eating steaks of different thicknesses. Therefore, to appeal to everyone, it is wise to cut steaks into assorted widths. I cut my steaks into three sizes: one-half, three-quarters, and one-inch thicknesses.

When cutting the hind legs, after you have removed the larger cuts mentioned above, revisit the rear leg again and trim off any and all meat left on it. You will end up with a surprising amount of tender pieces and strips of meat. A small amount of these tender portions can be tossed into the pile of meat heading to the grinder for chopped meat to make burgers and sausages. The very best thing to do with these small very palatable chunks or strips of rump meat is to prepare them as Kate does. Using a butcher knife, Kate slices the meat into ½- to ¾-inch-thick round steaks. They can be used as steaks or pounded thinner into cutlets. If they are made into cutlets, then they are dipped in an egg batter, floured, breaded with Italian breadcrumbs, and fried or baked into Italian-style cutlets.

During the butchering process, set these pieces aside into a separate plastic tub. Eventually the pieces will be shrink-wrapped and frozen as one-pound portions. Once they are defrosted, they can be used to make a delicious Asian stir-fry, quick fried in oil and/or butter, and the larger strips used in stroganoff and other similar dishes that require extra tender meat—yummy.

Photo credit: Kerry Swendsen, www.deerdummy.com

Once the rear leg is broken into different cuts, take the time to go back to the rear leg bones, which contain some of the best meat on the deer, and trim away any remaining meat. You'll end up with a lot of tender chunks that can make excellent ground or stew meat.

What the Pros Say

The advice given by many professional butchers and chefs is to allow the knife blade to closely move along the bones, which act as a road map that makes butchering a deer or beef carcass easier. Three such pros with the same mindset are listed below, with one taking the adage *"follow the bone"* to new heights. Each of them shares decades of experience, skills, and advice with anyone interested in DIY butchering of deer. Within each of their highly informative and instructional DVDs are hours of how-to video on this subject, which anyone who has an interest in butchering deer at home will enjoy and learn from.

Kerry Swendsen is the fifth generation of meat cutters in his family that began in Denmark. Swendsen's company is called DeerDummy. com. His company offers many useful butchering items, including boning knives, butcher mats, and other products. His instructional "Follow the Bone Deer Cutting" DVD includes sage advice on how to butcher a deer. One of my favorite products from Deer Dummy is a very useful poster that doubles as both a meat-cutting mat and a highly informational reference poster. It is called the Deer Dummy Deer Cutting Mat. It was primarily designed to be used as a large meat-cutting mat (twenty-seven by forty inches) that lays flat, giving the DIY butcher a clean, specific area to cut meat on. The mat includes micro-ban protection with built-in properties that inhibit the growth of stains and odor-causing bacteria. It is constructed of commercial-grade HDPE polyethylene. It will also not dull knife blades when cutting meat on it. After its use as a cutting mat, it can be washed down with warm water and soap and/or bleach and warm water. It can then be rolled up and stored away until needed.

Photo credit: Kerry Swendsen, www.deerdummy.com

This mat's sharp images provide a highly visible instructional pictorial step-by-step butchering guide that illustrates countless cuts of venison.

John Person—a.k.a. **JB**—is the president of Game Butchers, LLC. JB's father John Person, who processed venison, beef, hogs, lamb, and veal, started the business fifty years ago. Today, the business is "focused on hunter's venison" and JB, his brothers Jim and Jeff, and his mother Jan carry on the tradition. JB has been a professional game butcher for more than forty years. His trademark is that he provides the best possible cuts from each and every deer he butchers for his customers. The company sells a line of farm-raised venison products, including cutlets, roasts, cube steaks, stew meat, ground venison, boneless round steaks, country sausage, Italian sweet and hot sausage, kielbasa, hot dogs, bratwurst, pepperoni sticks, and the most mouthwatering line of venison jerky that our family has ever had the pleasure of eating. He also has a line of tasty seasonings and other butchering products. John and his sons also produced an excellent, informative two-part DVD series called, "Game Butchers–After the Hunt" and "Game Butchers–White-tailed Deer Processing," that includes more than 121 minutes of easy-to-understand and follow instructional information. Visit their site for more information on their farm-raised venison, services, and products at www.game-butcher.com

Photo credit: www.GameButchers.com

This two-hour series was produced by John and his sons. It is a trove of instructional information. The easy-to-follow instructions will have you cutting up meat like a pro in no time at all.

Another butchering pro is **Brad Lockwood,** who has more than twenty-five years of experience in the meat-processing industry. Brad has done everything from owning and operating his own federally inspected meat-processing plant, to holding the office of president of the Pennsylvania Association of Meat Processors.

Brad produced several outstanding informational butchering DVDs. One DVD is a nine-hour compilation, beginning with the basics of deer processing, quartering, and de-boning, sausage and jerky making, marinating, and a bonus DVD from his television show, *The Love of the Hunt* TV series. It includes hunts for elk, moose, mule deer, antelope, bear, Africa plains game, turkeys, and whitetails.

Brad's company is exceptionally innovative when it comes to anything related to deer processing, including portable walk-in coolers, hide rippers, single S-hooks, meat trees, and DVDs. One of the most inventive products in the Koola Buck line is the antimicrobial game spray and antimicrobial deer bags. If, after reading this book, you get the point about NOT allowing insects and other vermin to infest your meat, then you will want to check out Koola Buck's antimicrobial sprays and game bags post-haste at www.koolabuck.com. I highly recommend the use of these products.

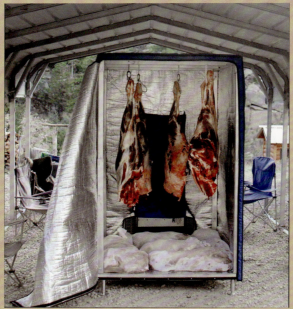

Photo credit: Brad Lockwood.

One of the most important elements to better tasting venison is being able to keep the carcass fresh, cool, and free of vermin. Koola Buck's coolers have all the features of permanent walk-in coolers, but they include the added value of being portable.

Photo credit: Kerry Swendsen.

Deer processing begins with using the right knives. This six-inch Deer Dummy boning knife is easy to control around every bone and is balanced well. It will help you cut every bit of delectable venison from your deer quickly and precisely. Visit www. deerdummy.com for more information.

Terrence John Daly—a.k.a. **TJ**—is the head butcher/supervisor at New York Custom Processing. He has been professionally processing beef for thirteen years. TJ's experience also includes processing lamb, hogs, and veal. When it comes to processing beef, TJ is known as a perfectionist and will go to no ends to make sure each cut is "precisely made to NYCP's client's exact specifications and satisfaction." TJ is widely recognized as one of the top-notch butchers in the Northeast.

Additionally, TJ is an avid deer and other wild-game hunter. At the early age of ten years old, TJ was taught how to butcher deer by his grampa, Charles Crowe, and his uncle, Richard VanDyke. Since that time, he has processed countless deer for his family and his hunting friends. When it comes to butchering venison, TJ is no less a perfectionist than when he processes beef. He demands that each cut of venison is treated just as carefully as the high-end beef he processes.

Darren Hazen is a local DIY butcher with decades of experience and over the last decade he has passed his skills on to his son Deven, who helps Darren butcher dozens of deer each season. What began as a family tradition has grown exponentially for Darren, who now regularly butchers deer not only for his family but as a favor for many friends as well. Darren uses much of his personal meat to create different types of delicious summer sausage, Italian and breakfast sausage, as well other types of sausages. He is a skilled butcher who generously shares his butchering knowledge and talents with anyone who is willing to learn. His enthusiasm and passion for DIY butchering and sausage making is truly contagious.

Chapter 13

Butchering Loins and Ribs

When it comes to DIY butchering topics, the first subject that inevitably arises is what portions of the carcass provide the most tender and flavorful cuts. There should be absolutely no debate on this question, as the small tenderloins and the larger backstraps (a.k.a. loins, steaks, and the other less common names they go by) are the two utmost tender and scrumptious cuts on all North American antlered deer species (deer, moose, elk, and caribou).

Small Tenderloins

The small tenderloins are located inside along both sides of the backbone (spine). When it comes to talking about them on all species of deer, they are most often referred to as tenderloins. On a domestic beef, however, they are most commonly and correctly referred to as the beef tenderloins. On a deer carcass, the small tenderloins are found on the undersides of the spine within the chest cavity. The tenderloins can be compared in both

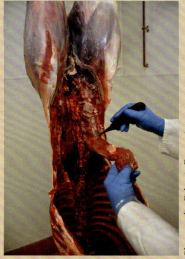

Cutting these two little gems of meat from the deer should not be missed. They are some of the tastiest and most tender of all the cuts on a deer's carcass.

their tenderness and delectability to the aforementioned tenderloins of domestic beef cattle. Most people who eat venison tenderloins claim, and rightfully so, they are equally mouthwatering and delicious when, just like beef, they are prepared correctly. The tenderloins are much smaller than the backstraps.

On the other hand, the two much larger and longer pieces of meat found at the top, exterior sides of the spine, lying just under the deer's hide, are commonly called backstraps. Mmmmm . . . backstraps. The matching parts of a deer's backstraps are the various cuts of prime steaks found on a domestic beef carcass. On a beef cow, though, they are more appropriately called

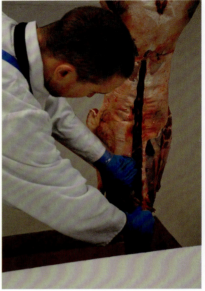

Photo credit: Fiduccia Enterprises.

The large backstraps rank high within the three most tender and best-tasting cuts of venison.

the T-bone steaks and porterhouse steaks. The backstraps, like the mini-tenderloins, are equally tender tasting and delicious when compared to each other. Both cuts are so tender it really isn't necessary to tenderize them through aging (wet or dry) or by soaking them in a marinade.

There are a couple of different methods that can be used to remove these two tasty cuts of venison (tenderloins and backstraps). This is contingent on whether the deer is going to be butchered bone out or bone in. By now, you know I unconditionally prefer to bone out my deer or other big-game carcasses. So, that is the way I am referring to the removal of the mini-tenderloins and backstraps here. You may recall, I covered the removal of them both briefly in an earlier chapter on quartering. Nevertheless, because these cuts are so delectable, a more complete recap about their removal is certainly warranted.

The removal of the small tenderloins is easy. To preserve their flavor and tenderness, they should be removed from the deer immediately after the carcass has been hung on the game pole. No matter when you remove the mini tenderloins, taking them out of the deer is always done the same way.

I took this dandy 12-point on our farm in 2016. The mini-tenderloins were taken out shortly after hanging the deer. After that, we caped him and placed the carcass in an antimicrobial game bag. The next day the deer was processed (butchered).

A reason to remove the tenderloins after field dressing the deer is because the small tenderloins, unlike the larger backstraps, do not have a protective hide covering. Therefore, if the deer is hung on the game pole for more than one day, or it is not going to be processed for a few days or more, the small tenderloins will develop a crusty, hard casing on their surface. And the longer they remain in the carcass, the worse the coating becomes. Once they are covered with a coating, it is an absolute must that you will have to carefully trim the entire glazed-over casing completely off both small tenderloins. Yup, you probably guessed it. That will certainly result in a loss in their overall size and also impact their flavor and tenderness.

Because I generally hang my deer on the game pole within an hour or so after shooting it, I almost always remove the small tenderloins directly after the deer is safely secured and hanging. Once they are out, I trim away the fat, silverskin, and any other connective tissue and place the tenderloins into a Zip-lock bag. Like many other hunters, I enjoy cooking and eating the small tenderloins within a day or two after taking the deer. If we don't eat them soon, they get vacuum-sealed and frozen.

Here's how to remove the mini-tenderloins. These two small strips of meat can be gently coaxed (pulled) free from the body cavity. However, in order to preserve as much meat as possible, I recommend removing them using the tip of a sharp boning knife. It doesn't take much to cut them free from the deer's backbone. Taking the two smaller tenderloins out of the body cavity is as straightforward as that.

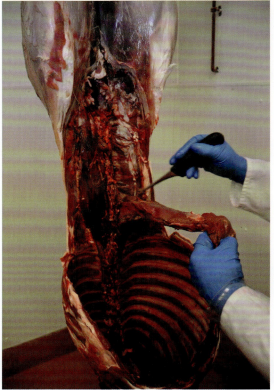

When done correctly and with a sharp boning knife, the small tenderloins can be extracted in less than fifteen minutes. With a little experience, it can be done in even less time.

Photo credit: Fiduccia Enterprises.

Large Tenderloins, a.k.a. Backstraps

The two large backstraps (loins) are found on the exterior of the vertebral column, just under the deer's hide. They are adjacent to the backbone, running from just behind the front shoulder down all the way to where the back legs start. Removing the two large backstraps, requires more attention than taking out the two small tenderloins. A majority of hunters want to take the backstraps out in one long piece, as do most professional and DIY butchers. To extract them in long strips, use a sharp boning knife with a flexible tip that will bend as it moves past the bones. Place the tip of the knife directly against the backbone and begin to slowly and carefully filet between the bone and the meat.

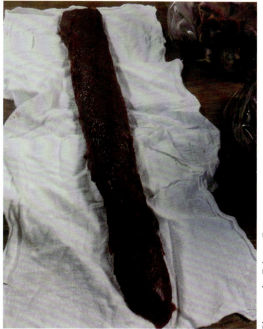

Photo credit: Fiduccia Enterprises.

A single backstrap can be cut up into a dozen or more one-inch-thick steaks. If the cuts are less than one-inch thick, one backstrap will provide even more than a dozen steaks and even some cutlets as well.

While doing this, you may feel your blade bounce or skip along; that is a good thing, as it is gliding over the deer's vertebrae, which means you are following the bone and removing a majority of the backstrap meat. Continue to cut down until you reach the area of the front shoulder and top of the neck. As you cut slowly and carefully, keep lifting the meat. Gently pull it away with your free hand, while gradually filleting the backstrap out of the deer's spinal pocket and rib cage until the entire piece of backstrap is removed. Repeat the same technique on the other side of the spinal column to remove the other backstrap meat.

When done properly, the two backstraps will end up being two long pieces of delectable meat. Once they are removed, trim away the silverskin, fat and connective tissue. Before beginning to cut (slice) them into steaks or cutlets, remove any small pieces of hair with a damp cloth.

Generally, it is recommended to cut each piece of meat into one-inch thick slices (although some suggest even thicker pieces than that). Kate and I like to cut them thinner, as they will cook more quickly and taste even more delicious. Another way we enjoy them is to butterfly each cut into a very thin cutlet that can either be breaded and/or quickly pan sautéed in a very hot skillet, as you would a beef steak. As you reach the end of a long backstrap, start to make the smaller cuts slightly thicker. They can be made a little larger by gently pounding them flat or butterflying them.

I shudder when I think about the other meat-cutting method some hunters use backstraps for: They cut them into bone in steaks (chops). Not only is this a much a less delectable way to use one of the two most scrumptious cuts of meat on the deer, it also requires a lot more time and work and, more

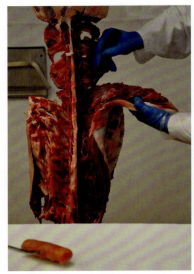

By following the bone, DIY butchers will retain a maximum amount of meat. This will also reduce the chances of accidentally cutting into meat that wasn't supposed to be cut into.

It's easy to see how a backstrap from an adult deer can end up providing dozens of one-inch mouthwatering steaks.

Photo credit: Fiduccia Enterprises.

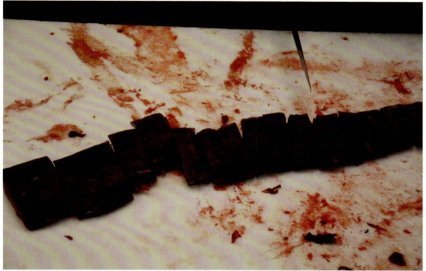

Pictured here are different size cuts of steaks from the backstrap. The thicker pieces on the left can be cooked like filet mignons. Other cuts such as one-inch steaks and smaller cuts can be butterflied and gently pounded into cutlets.

important, it requires sawing the carcass in half, down the centerline of the entire backbone.

You may recall my earlier comments about the concerns of CWD when cutting through deer bones. While writing this book, there was a news item on my cell phone titled "Zombie Deer." It said researchers are worried that a brain illness known as "zombie deer" caused by CWD could infect humans. The main focus of the article was to avoid the possibility of contacting CWD from the venison of an infected deer. Although that the chances of that happening are extremely slim, it is wise when butchering deer to avoid contact with the deer's brain and fluids from the spine or bones. Hence, I don't cut through deer bones. By

This photo was taken in the 1990s, before CWD was an issue as it is today. Back then, cutting through the bone to make rib chops was not worrisome. Nowadays, the USDA does not advise not taking this risk.

the way, an important sidebar here, as of this writing, no human has *ever* been infected with Chronic Wasting Disease from a deer.

Lastly, let's touch on the importance of trimming these two cuts well. It will help to further maximize the flavor of the mini-tenderloins and backstraps by carefully trimming them free of silverskin, fat, and any other connective tissue. This is particularly true if both the small tenderloins and the larger backstraps are going to be eaten soon after they are cut. If they are going to be vacuum-sealed and frozen for future use, however, then they don't have to be trimmed quite as carefully during the processing stage. By leaving a little fat and connective tissue on the cuts, some meat experts claim the fat will help protect the cuts when in the freezer.

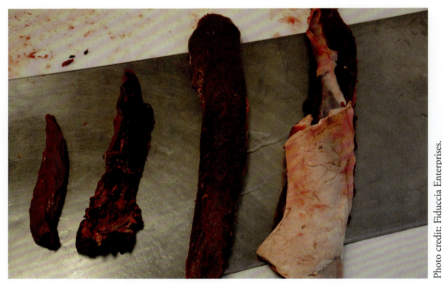

Photo credit: Fiduccia Enterprises.

From right to left, untrimmed and trimmed backstraps and tenderloins. It's plain to see how important it is to properly trim these pieces.

So there you have it. Ways to remove, butcher, and trim the tenderloins and backstraps—voted the most tender and flavorful cuts of venison by hunters and DIY butchers in the know!

The Ribs

Now we get to the rib ends, which in reality contain less meat than most of the other cuts. Let's face it, venison ribs simply don't taste like beef and pork ribs, and the fact is that they never will no matter how they are prepared. That is why a lot of hunters don't like venison ribs. In fact, many times, particularly on a fawn or yearling deer, the rib sections are given away or, worse yet, discarded. That is a mistake. While the meat isn't the finest cut on the deer, it can be set aside in the bins to be ground into burger and/or sausage meat.

One reason for the ribs not tasting all that good is that most hunters fail to cook off the tallow prior to finishing off the ribs on a grill or in a broiler. By pre-cooking the ribs using a sous-vide or any other pre-cooked manner, it will substantially eliminate most, if not all, of the foul taste caused by the tallow.

Place the ribs in the oven or broiler on a wired meat-cooking rack on a low to medium heat for forty-five to sixty minutes. The tallow and other fat will melt from the ribs as they cook. Drain the fat from the bottom of the pan a couple of times during the cooking process, as the melted fat has an odor that can permeate the cooking ribs. In about an hour, the tallow and other fat will be completely melted. Now they can be finished off by basting them with any type of barbeque or other type sauce preferred and cooking them on a grill or in a broiler or oven.

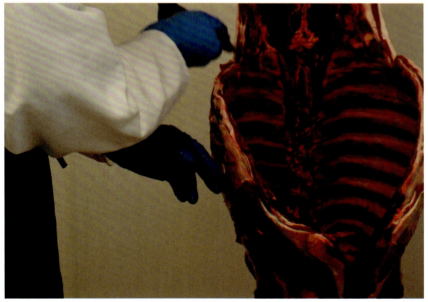

Photo credit: Fiduccia Enterprises.

Don't discard deer ribs. Instead, trim them well for meat that will go into burger and sausage. Or, the ribs can be made on the grill when prepared and cooked properly.

With that all said, and no matter how venison ribs are prepared, they will never end up tasting as scrumptious as beef or pork ribs do. Cooked as suggested above, though, they will be surprisingly better tasting than most hunters think they will turn out. There you have it. Venison ribs anyone?

Photo credit: Fiduccia Enterprises.

Here are other types of cuts that can be made from backstraps.

Chapter 14

Tenderizing Venison

———

Years ago, the meat of any game animal was termed as "venison." *Webster's Dictionary* defines wild venison as: "Venison originally described meat of any game animal killed by hunting, and was applied to any animal from the families Cervidae (deer), Leporidae (hares), and Suidae (wild pigs), and certain species of the genus Capra (goats and ibex). In Southern Africa, the word *venison* refers to the meat of antelope."

Over the last few decades, however, the terminology has changed somewhat. For a majority of hunters today, the term venison isn't applied to all wild game any longer. Instead the jargon (venison) derives solely from belonging to the five North American deer species, commonly known as white-tailed deer, mule deer, elk, moose, and caribou. No matter how you cut it (forgive the pun), the meat from these deer, both large and small, is called venison.

Now the conundrum. When two pieces of raw wild venison and farm-raised domestic beef are compared to one another, in particular the loins, they can look similar. Therefore, when wild venison is being prepared by some hunters, and particularly by non-hunters, they often tend to use the cooking methods of beef for wild venison. Once this thought takes hold, it subliminally enters the mind that wild venison can be prepared (cooked) exactly like domestic meat from beef. Although both wild venison and beef cattle meat can look the same, the fact is the only thing they really have in common is that they are both considered red meat.

When it comes to cooking beef and wild venison, they are going to end up tasting significantly different from one another if they are cooked in the

Photo credit: Fiduccia Enterprises.

Today venison is a much broader term than it used to be in the early part of the century. It encompasses all North American deer species including the largest deer of all: moose. I took this big bull in Newfoundland at Red Indian Lake Outfitting (www.redindianake.com).

same way. By the way, I use the word "wild" here because farm-raised venison (farm-raised deer are fed a regimented and highly nutritious diet) does taste different from free-ranging venison. I want to make sure the two are not confused. Going forward in this chapter, however, when I refer to cooking or discussing venison, it refers to meat from wild deer, not farm-raised deer.

The major difference between beef and venison is almost entirely related to the amount of fat content of each animal. Fat content, and/or the lack of fat accumulated in an animal's meat, is mostly responsible for how its meat will taste when cooked. In fact, it can be said that fat may be totally accountable for the tenderness, flavor, texture, and, most of all, the appealing tastefulness of beef or, for some people, the lack of appeal for venison. Fat (more often referred to as marbling) is a key factor in how beef and venison must be cooked differently.

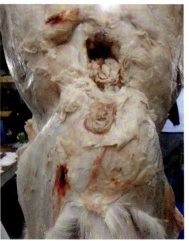

The external fat seen here does nothing to impart better flavor to the deer's meat. Only intramuscular fat aids in giving deer meat a better taste.

There should be no doubt that the mistake in believing that venison can be prepared and cooked like beef will inevitably lead to venison tasting less than enjoyable, especially to those who have never eaten it before. When people cook venison like beef, they

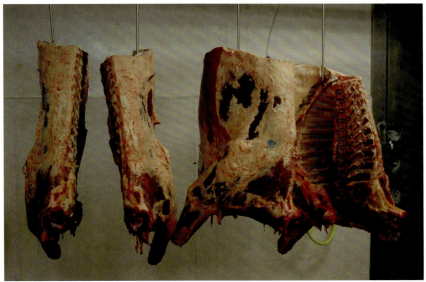

Unlike the external fat found on deer, the external fat on beef complements the intramuscular fat by imparting the all-familiar, delicious flavor of domestic beef.

expect it to taste like beef. That one factor predominantly accounts for why many venison meals are ruined. Venison doesn't taste like beef, and no matter how you prepare it, it *never* will. But that isn't to imply it can't taste as delicious as beef, because it indeed can and does.

Meat experts assert that the tissue structure of beef is moderately fine grained and marbled. On the other hand, venison is more coarsely grained, very lean, and is sparsely marbled. If at all, the marbling is hardly visible. This can be directly contributed to the deer's wild diet, which is a chief factor in giving venison a different full-bodied flavor than beef.

The amount of fat (marbling) content in beef allows it to be grilled, baked, broiled, roasted, fried, sautéed, and/or barbecued over heat much longer than venison and still end up being tender and full of flavor when served, even when cooked to a well-done state. Because venison is very lean and has no significant amount of marbling, its meat has no lubricating fat to percolate all the way through the soft tissue fibers and break them down.

Tenderizing

There is a lot of scientific information related to the subject of tenderizing venison, but in the end, cooking venison as long as you would cook a cut of beef will always result in a poor tasting piece of venison. In order to have the most savory and delicious venison meals, the meat must always be cooked no more than medium and, better yet, medium-rare to rare. Overcook it, and it is destined to receive poor reviews.

But fret not, as there are other resolves to tenderizing venison. But it is *crucially* important for me to make this point here about tenderizing venison. Venison can be cooked in many mouthwatering recipes without worrying about tenderizing it first. Using the advice about not overcooking it is a *major solution* to achieving delectable tasting venison. However, sauces and seasonings, like those often included to enhance a beef dish, will also augment a venison dish.

A popular way to quickly tenderize any meat is to pound it thin and then poke holes in it with a sharp instrument. Better yet, once any piece of meat has been lightly pounded, it can be further tenderized using a tool called a Jaccard tenderizer. A Jaccard tenderizer has dozens of sharp, pointed pieces of steel (teeth) that, when pressed down from the handle, neatly puncture into the meat, cutting through any connective tissue and breaking the protein strands. This tool will help to tenderize even some of the toughest

Photo credit: Fiduccia Enterprises.

The holes in the meat were made by a Jaccard tenderizer tool. Kate is preparing these for our traditional opening evening appetizer. Other companies that make professional tenderizers include Special, Norpro, Concle, Flytt, and Mercier.

pieces of venison, beef, and other meats. When used on prime cuts, it works even better. However, the user must be mindful that poking so many extra holes into a piece of meat will allow the meat to be cooked more quickly. Allowances for this fact should be kept in mind when cooking. A Jaccard tool performs flawlessly and is easily broken down to be cleaned.

Larding

You can supplement fat to venison using a larding method as well. Larding is the cooking technique of inserting strips or pieces of fat into a piece of meat that doesn't have much fat of its own, like venison. The added fat melts and keeps the venison meat from drying out. When larding meat, a needle is typically used to pierce the meat and sew in the strand(s) of fat, which are usually bacon or pork fat. As an FYI here, it is a long-held myth that braising or even boiling meat will keep it moist.

Barding

Another method is called barding. Barding is simply done by adding a thin slice of fat, or better yet bacon, to meat. It is usually secured to a roast

Photo credit: Canstock.

Wrapping meat (venison or traditional meats) with slices of pork bacon and/or thin slices of beef fat is called barding. Here, venison meat rolls are wrapped thoroughly in bacon. Larding, on the other hand, is when small chunks of fat are put into the meat.

or placed around other pieces of venison (securing it with a toothpick or wrapping it around the meat with butcher's string) to prevent the venison from drying out while cooking. Many chefs and cooks claim that any piece of meat that is wrapped with fat can be termed as "barding."

Marinades

Other than adding fat, how else can you tenderize venison? The answer is by using any of the literally countless marinade recipes that are readily available in books or online. Search online for marinades for venison and you can spend a lot of time browsing all the recipes that come up. A marinade is a liquid bath that venison cuts can be soaked in for various lengths of time prior to them being cooked. A marinade can also be infused or injected into a cut of venison. All the venison roasts from a deer are the cuts of meat that are most frequently drenched in a marinade. Many other venison cuts also benefit from being saturated in a marinade as well.

Photo credit: Fiduccia Enterprises.

There are countless products to use to tenderize or marinade venison.

Keep in mind that a marinade can either impart a flavor to the meat or both impart flavor and tenderize the meat.

The Scientific Gobbledygook

As I noted above, there is a lot of science "gobbledygook" about what makes any meat tender, including venison. I generally like to indulge in all things related to the science, biology, behavior, and everything else about white-tailed deer. In this instance, though, it can get downright complicated and, to a degree, boring, so I'll try to keep it as brief and interesting as possible.

By now we know that marbling is an essential factor in making meat tender. But it doesn't present the complete scientific picture about how meat becomes tender. So here we go. Researchers and meat professionals state that there are twenty-five different categories of enzymes found in all types of meats.

But what are enzymes, you might ask. Well, according to the experts, they are chemical ferments that through a process known as oxidation, work on proteins, carbohydrates, and fats in meats. They work to break

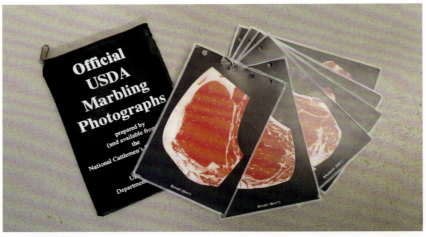

Photo credit: USDA.

These images show the various levels of marbling in beef. In venison, the marbling is so slight that it's rarely as visible as it is in beef. Venison marbling is present intramuscularly. Most free-ranging deer rarely have marbling due to their diet.

down connective tissue, reducing it to a gelatinous consistency. This biological process makes meat not only tender, it also heightens its flavor and succulence by releasing water in the meat.

Because of differences in their chemical constitution and the associated activity of enzymes, animal fats differ considerably in their propensity to oxidize. Venison fat oxidizes slowly because there is not much interstitial fat (marbling) to begin with. Consequently, when cooked like beef, venison will be tough tasting. Hence the benefit of using the above-mentioned larding or barding methods to cook venison. My favorite is using bacon, but beef fat, salt pork, or beef suet can also be used.

But this section is dedicated to using a combination of ingredients to create delectable marinades. Again, as I stated earlier, there are literally countless marinade recipes to use. There are also dozens of combinations of ingredients commonly found in marinades, and each adds different flavors to the venison.

Generally, they all share a common thread of having a highly acidic or enzyme-type ingredient (usually wine, salt brine, vinegar, etc.). All of these ingredients help dramatically speed up the slow enzymatic oxidation process that breaks down a meat's connective tissue and makes it tender.

Photo credit: Fiduccia Enterprises.

Kate celebrates the taking of her buck (the one in the middle) with The Nerd Gang. From left to right: Eric Schultz (CIA analyst), our son Cody (PhD candidate), Alex Brozdowski (executive consultant, Deloitte), Dr. Victor Schultz (MIT post-doc), William Schultz (Naval Academy officer), and Kate.

Using different marinades to enhance the delicacy of venison is an outstanding solution. Or you can appreciate the unique and savory flavor of the venison without doing much more than not overcooking it. I can't tell you how many rave reviews Kate has had by our son's hunting buddies (Eric Schultz, Alex Brozdowski, Dr. Victor Schultz, Brandt Kayser, William Schultz—a.k.a. "The Ultimate Nerd Gang") when she makes her famous "quick pan moose loin" appetizer on the evening of opening day.

Kate simply cuts very thin slices from a few pounds of backstraps and/ or tenderloins, gently pounds them thin, and places them in a pre-heated frying pan. The pan is lightly coated with pure top-grade canola oil. The venison is placed in the pan and sizzled in the oil for several seconds, then flipped for an additional few seconds as she quickly sprinkles each serving with nothing more than a little crushed sea-salt and freshly crushed black pepper. They hit the plate sizzling hot, nicely browned on each side, and medium-rare. All of us wait with our mouths watering as Kate keeps them coming until she is out of meat to cook.

Photo credit: Fiduccia Enterprises.

Kate is seasoning her famous Opening Day venison appetizer for The Nerd Gang with freshly ground pepper. The guys regularly consume an entire large backstrap before dinner! Note how thinly cut the meat is, making the cooking time only seconds long on each side. The dish is straightforward to make, but amazingly delicious.

Chapter 15

How to Convert Venison Meat Cuts to Ground

One of the most common cuts of meat requested by customers of certified meat-processing plants is ground meat. This is the case in many meat-processing facilities, including the more controlled plants that are USDA approved and monitored. Often, meat-processing owners and supervisors use what is technically referred to as a "cut sheet" when taking orders from clients. A cut sheet is the form that a customer fills out prior to their meat (pig, sheep, cull cow, etc.) being butchered. It describes in detail how the customer wants each and every cut of their beef or other domestic animal butchered. I am not recommending that DIY home butchers use such a detailed form, but it is wise to use an abbreviated cut sheet that includes all the different cuts you want to make during the butchering process. Every reliable deer-processing plant will have a hunter provide them information that they can put on their cut sheet. It helps to eliminate mistakes and helps the process move along in a timelier manner. It can provide the same benefits for the DIY home butcher. It helps keep everything on track.

A cut sheet is particularly important in most meat-processing plants because some clients may want their ground meat made from more of the prime cuts of the steer than the usual cuts used to make ground meat. Or, a customer may want the ground meat from the steer's loin cuts (ground sirloin) because he or she feels that that specific cut is going to be superior to the ground meat taken from the steer's lesser body parts (ground chuck).

NEW YORK CUSTOM PROCESSING, LLC   430 Rte. 8 Bridgewater, NY 13313   Tel - (315) 204-4084   Fax 4090
www.newyorkcustomprocessing.com

CUSTOM CUT SHEET

KILL - $100.00   *PROCESSING: $0.80/lb. & $0.85/lb. for Premium Cuts*

Shaved Steak/Fajitas/Patties Surcharge: $0.75/LB.

$25 per add'l cut instructions   *$2.05/box*   *$.38/lb. surcharge for "Retail" packaging of 1/package*
$20/order for supplemental labeling

Number of Beef: _____   Tag # _____   HCW: _____

FARMER   Name: _____   Phone: _____

Drop Off Date: _____/_____/_____   _____

PROCESSED FOR   Name: _____   Phone: _____

Processing Date: _____/_____/_____   Pick Up Date: _____/_____/_____

CHUCK

	CUT	WRAPPING		CUT	WRAPPING
Blade:			Arm:		
Brisket:			Shortribs:		
Hanger Steak:			Shanks:		

RIB

	CUT	WRAPPING		
Roasts:				
Steaks:				

LOIN   (if the animal is older than 30 mo., then the only options are Tenderloin Filet AND Top Loin)

	CUT	WRAPPING		CUT	WRAPPING
Tenderloin Filet:			Top Loin:		
T-Bone (<30 months)/Porterhouse:					

	CUT	WRAPPING		
Sirloin Steak:				

ROUND

	CUT	WRAPPING		CUT	WRAPPING
Sirloin Tip:			Top:		
Bottom:			Eye:		
Flank:			Liver:		
Tongue:			Heart:		
Bones:			Tail:		

Ground Beef/Stew Instructions: (standard packing is 2 lb. packs – surcharge of $0.50/lb. for 1 lb. packs)
_____

Additional Instructions: _____

This is a sample cut sheet from New York Custom Processing, LLC. It is simply meant to give you an idea what details are in a cut sheet. For the DIY butcher, a cut sheet doesn't have to be nearly as detailed as this. But, it is an excellent tool to help you save time and keep your butchering on track.

So when it comes to venison, the meat set aside to be used for ground can range from really flavorful parts of the carcass to less tasteful cuts (neck, shoulder, ribs, etc.). At our home, Kate uses ground meat for a lot of different recipes including burgers, meat loaf, chili, breakfast sausage, tacos, and many different types of casserole dishes. Since we enjoy Italian food, Kate also uses a lot of ground venison when she prepares meals like spaghetti and meatballs, between the layers of lasagna, in stuffed shells, manicotti (cheese stuffing and topped meat sauce), and other pasta dishes. Perhaps I have made the point now to help you recognize the significant versatility and value of ground venison.

The chopped meat coming out of the grinder has mixed with the fatty pork trimming (on the right) and special seasoning that Kate also uses in her "Hoochie Mamma Chili" recipe.

Photo credit: Fiduccia Enterprises.

When butchering the carcass, you should use two separate vats (bins) in which to place pieces of trimmed meat that are designated to become ground. The meat from the finer cuts of the carcass can be placed in vat "A" and the meat from the lesser cuts can be placed in vat "B." When the time comes to grind the meat, shrink wrap, and freeze it, the packages can be marked "A" and "B" ground. When time comes to cook the ground meat, you can then choose with confidence which package you want to use for the particular dishes you want to prepare.

Venison meat trimmings set aside for grinding into sausage meat are no different, so they too can be divided into two different vats. Some bulk sausage can be made into breakfast patties, some into traditional round sausage used for dinner meals or any of the Italian meals mentioned above. Sausage making is very flexible, and with a little work and creativity it can also be used to make a wide variety of sausages, including kielbasa, Polish sausage, summer sausage, salami, bologna, and much more. All of these can be frozen for long periods of time without going rancid (about a year or so).

This type of flexibility of ground meat product is why Kate tells me that sometimes even her most high-end clients request their entire steer or cull cow to be made into ground. It is also why many hunters do the same thing with their deer and other big-game animals.

Grinding Equipment

To be frank, the best way to grind any meat, including venison, is to use a quality electric meat grinder. There are a wide variety of different models, sizes, and brands available, at many different prices. Believe it or not, some grinders are still available with hand-cranks. They require a lot of work and a lot of extra time to grind meat. I would not recommend them.

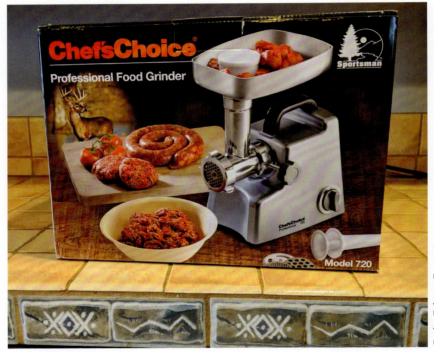

Credit: Fiduccia Enterprises.

When using a grinder, it pays big dividends to purchase one that will do the job reliably for many years. At a capacity of grinding three and one-half pounds per minute, it will serve the DIY butcher well.

If you enjoy ground venison, don't be a cheapskate when purchasing an electric meat grinder. Meat grinders/processing food units come basically in four categories: cheap units; home countertop models; larger, heavier, and much better made countertop grinders; and still larger stand-alone models. A good unit will have a reliable motor and appropriate voltage and/or horsepower. By using a quality-made grinder, you'll reap big dividends by insuring better-tasting ground meat. Remember this about purchasing meat grinders. If you buy a cheap unit, I also recommend that you have smoke alarms in your butchering area.

Realistically, if you are only going to grind less than fifteen to twenty pounds of venison trim a year, the second category type unit will serve you well and will end up being a sensible investment. You can expect units of this category to sell from about $200 to $500 depending on the bells and whistles they offer. If you grind twenty-five pounds or more, then the units in the third category are what you will need.

Then there are the commercially made grinders that were used when I worked at Tommaso's Butcher shop in my teens. They are usually free-standing meat grinders. Their electric motors are rated by horsepower, not voltage. They are mostly used in meat-processing plants, restaurants, retail

Photo credit: Fiduccia Enterprises.

The DIY home butcher who grinds less than twenty pounds of venison a year won't need more than a home countertop model grinder. However, it may be wise to buy a heavier duty countertop grinder, especially if your DIY interests expand.

butcher shops, some seasonal deer processing places, and only the most serious of DIY home butchers. They should only be considered by the DIY home butcher if the intention is to grind more than seventy-five pounds or more of venison into ground meat per season. These units can retail from about $1,000 to $1,500, and you can buy them at restaurant supply houses. Sometimes these houses will also sell pre-owned units that will cost less than the new models. Or you can occasionally find a pre-owned affordable unit for sale from a restaurant or butcher shop that is upgrading to a newer unit.

Another consideration when purchasing a meat grinder, a.k.a. food processing device (mentioned in the third category above), is the weight of the unit. A heavy meat grinder, eight to ten pounds or more, won't "walk-off" the work area bench or the kitchen counter as you grind up your venison trim. Despite their hi-tech looks, meat grinders are no longer as cumbersome or difficult to use as they used to be. The trimmings set aside for ground are simply put into the top of the grinder and then fed through cutting devices.

Most quality meat grinders have removable face plates and interchangeable disks with various sized holes. For instance, the Williams-Sonoma full-size meat grinder/food processor model 720 is available at Chef's Choice (chefschoice.com/food grinders). It comes with a large die-cast metal hopper and three grinding plates (3mm, 4.5mm, and 8mm). This 400-watt electric meat grinder packs heavy-duty grinding power into a compact, easy-to-use machine that is convenient to use in a home kitchen or at the work site of your DIY butchering area. It will make short work (it grinds up three and one-half pounds of meat per minute) of the venison trimmings you are grinding to make meatballs, burgers, meatloaf, casseroles, tacos, sausages, and more.

What I find most convenient about this unit is the fact that it has a reverse setting to release any potential clogs. At ten pounds fourteen ounces, it is heavy enough to stay exactly where you place it as it grinds up the meat. This model has a cast-iron corrosion-free design and resettable motor overload protection. Its powerful DC motor makes the unit durable and rugged, and it delivers long-lasting performance. This model retails for about $225. See the sidebar for other grinders.

One of my other favorite meat grinders is the RedHead Big Bite Electric Meat Grinder by LEM Products. It is available from Bass Pro Shops (www.basspro.com). This unit will make short work of large piles of meat

Photo credit: Fiduccia Enterprises.

This Chef's Choice model comes with the attachments seen here and more are available as well.

in your kitchen or other butchering areas. The RedHead Big Bite Electric Meat Grinder is specifically designed to offer more meat grinding capacity. Big Bite models feature several design improvements to handle larger pieces of venison and other meats and will grind that "faster than ever before." They are also specially designed to be long-lasting grinders that combine an enhanced, permanently lubricated motor with all-metal gears and roller bearings for quieter, superior power and performance. I also like the fact that the RedHead Big Bite's rugged design includes a solid stainless steel housing, meat pan, grinder head, auger, grinding knife and plates, that provide DIY butchers and other users with years of dependable performance. The Big Bite Meat Grinder series also features an expanded head with a rifling pattern that allows it to accept larger pieces of meat and pushes the meat forward with less effort and less waste. The longer auger works with the head that allows for faster seconds grinds. The RedHead Big Bite grinders are indeed powerful DIY butchering tools as well as in-home meat grinders.

There is another meat grinder for the DIY butcher who gets really involved in this hobby and butchers not only his own deer, but those of his family and friends as well. Obviously, the more deer you cut, the

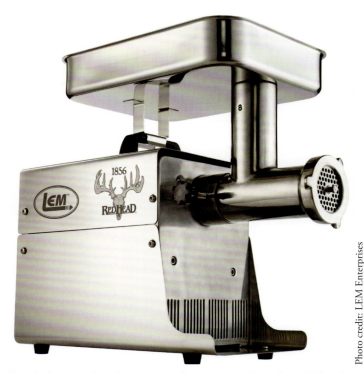

Photo credit: LEM Enterprises

The whole point about buying a quality meat grinder is for DIY butchers to not only lessen their work load, but also to produce high quality ground meat, making this unit a must-have tool in any DIY work area.

more meat you'll be passing through a grinder. Cabela's makes a line of heavy-duty professional-grade grinders in the Carnivore series. Their largest unit has a 1.75-hp motor and will grind nineteen to twenty-three pounds per minute. It retails for about $749. Cabela's 1.5-hp Carnivore grinder moves fourteen to eighteen pounds per minute and retails for $649; and their smaller 1.0-hp Carnivore grinder passes eleven to thirteen pounds of meat per minute and retails for $499. These are units for the serious DIY butcher who has a budget that allows for the purchasing of high-end professional equipment like this. For

Photo credit: Cabela's.

For those DIYers who regularly butcher several deer a season, Cabela's line of heavy-duty high-end grinders are workhorse models. Their top-end model seen here can grind up to twenty-three pounds of meat per minute.

more information about Cabela's line of Carnivore meat grinders, which all come with a lifetime guarantee, visit www.cabelas.com.

I could go on and on about what models and prices are available, but the best advice I can offer is to do your homework before purchasing a grinder. Prices can range from $100 to more than $1000. If you are only going to make a small amount of ground meat—say less than twenty pounds—an intermediate-size electric grinder (with a 110-volt motor) will do the job just fine. They generally cost about $140 to $175. If, on the other hand, you grind up forty or more pounds of deer meat, then I would say it is practical to invest the money and buy a top-of-the-line home grinder. Lastly, if, like many hunters, you dedicate the entire deer to ground meat, then a professional model should be on your agenda. As mentioned, they can cost anywhere from $1,000 to $1,500 or more.

Maintenance

I like to say take care of your equipment and it will take care of you. That goes ten-fold for a meat grinder. Although the quality models rarely need servicing, all grinders, no matter how high end they are, require regular cleaning. I'll repeat that: REGULAR cleaning. Many moons ago, when I was about fifteen years old, I worked in an ice cream shop. We had a soft ice cream machine that had to be broken down (totally disassembled) after each day and completely cleaned before we could use it the following day. A meat grinder is exactly the same. Cleaning not only keeps them working well, but is also important from a health standpoint. Meat that is left in the blades of a grinder will go rancid quickly, and you don't want to mix that into the new meat you are grinding.

Photo credit: Fiduccia Enterprises.

Clean the machine thoroughly after each and every use. Carefully wash out all the parts, including the entire hopper, feed screw, and cutting blade in hot soapy water. It should go without saying, but don't submerse any of the electric grinder's motor in water.

They say cleanliness is next to godliness. Believe this. When it comes to keeping grinder and knives clean, when grinding venison, nothing can be more applicable than that saying. Always use food service gloves to keep germs from your hands out of the mix.

Do that and you will either fry or kill the machine. Simply wash the outside of the housing with a damp cloth. Since the blades are made of metal, they must be lubricated before putting the grinder away for an extended period so that none of the metal meat-cutting parts rust. Give them a light coating with vegetable oil or, better yet, mineral oil.

Grind it Up, Deer Hunter

Making ground meat is one of the more enjoyable parts of home butchering. Even a first-timer can do a professional job. For the best tasting ground, it is recommended that you get a small quantity of beef suet or beef fat. Beef suet is said to be comparable to deer tallow. It contains a concentrated, white, lard type of fat found in layers around the kidneys of the cow, down both sides of its back, and across the rump. It is very inexpensive

Photo credit: Mike Ring.

This is the way family and friends can share time enjoying home processing of deer. The ground meat that they are making is destined for burgers, meatloaf, chili, meatballs, and more.

to purchase, costing less than fifty cents a pound. Some butchers and processing plants will provide it for a lot less, and they may even give it to you for free. Beef fat lies closer to the carcass meat, beneath the suet, and therefore is not quite so thick. It commonly comes from the excess fat trimmed off cuts by the butchers during their final trimming process.

If you put a large portion of your venison, or even the majority of it, into ground, you will need a lot of suet or beef fat. The suggested ratio is three parts venison to one part suet and/or fat, which is a 75/25 ratio. Although some hunters weigh the meat and fat in order to be sure the ratio is correct, the fact is that is truly unnecessary, as you don't have to be worried about being

Photo credit: Fiduccia Enterprises.

Here we are mixing fatty pork (pork meat and fat already mixed together) into the ground venison. This batch will be mixed by hand with seasonings to make sausage.

that precise. Since venison and suet have about the same weight-to-volume concentration, it's easy to eyeball what three parts venison to one part suet/beef fat looks like.

Plan to buy your suet/beef fat early. Don't wait until deer season starts, as by then other hunters will also be looking for it. Think about how much you will need and then place an order before deer season with a local beef-processing plant, the local butcher, or the meat department in Walmart or similar stores. If you buy too much, it is cheap enough to dispose of the extra. For instance, if the entire deer is going to be used for burger, it will require about twenty-five to thirty pounds of fat or suet. Although suet will work, I prefer using beef fat as it is considerably more tender than suet and makes better-tasting burger. Try to get beef fat trimmings first. If that fails, go with the suet.

As I said earlier, you will want to work with very cold venison when grinding your meat. That way the blade of the grinder can cut the meat much more efficiently. If the meat is warm (even room temperature), it will have a propensity to get spongy and mushy and will be more difficult to put through the grinder. So, before grinding the meat, place it in covered bowl(s) in a refrigerator overnight. That will make the meat cold enough to move through the grinder without any problems. If you're running short on time, place the meat in a freezer for fifteen to thirty minutes which should be enough time for the meat to get thoroughly chilled down and easier to work through the grinder. Be wise about how long you leave your trimmings lying out. Once any meat is left out too long, and the temperatures exceed 40°F, you risk having bacteria multiply on the meat (there is always a tiny amount of bacteria on all meat that is being butchered, be it domestic or game—cooking kills most if not a majority of all bacteria). This is another good reason for working with very cold meat.

Once the meat is cold, cut up your suet or beef fat into two-inch pieces. These will pass through the grinder much faster and easier than larger portions of suet and fat. As the suet and/or beef fat passes through the coarse grinding plate, place them in a cold large tray or bowl. Next, feed the chilled venison through the same coarse plate. Feed pieces of meat no larger than a lemon through the grinder, as anything larger will be problematic.

After the suet and venison have each been ground through the coarse grinding plate, they should be placed on a clean work surface. Next, thoroughly mix the meat and the suet and/or fat together with your hands (that are hopefully covered with food service gloves), until they are completely

Photo credit: Fiduccia Enterprises.

When it comes to maintaining a grinder, it's crucial to keep the cutting blades and all the other parts in spic and span condition.

blended together. Then remove the coarse grinding plate and put in a medium-size grinding plate and run the mixed burger, suet, and/or fat through the grinder plate again.

It should be noted, however, that most professional butchers agree that the ground meat should be fed through the grinder at least two to four times in order to produce various textures of the ground product. For instance, a breakfast sausage or a meat loaf should not be made with heavy or thick ground meat that has only been put through the grinder twice. A two-time pass through is more appropriate to produce burger or bulk sausage of various textures.

By following this procedure, the ground meat should have the appearance and consistency that most DIY butchers strive to achieve. It will—or at least it should—look almost identical to store-bought burger meat. If it doesn't, it can be sent through the grinder a third time to achieve a finer texture. Now you have some quality ground venison that can be used in any recipe that you could use with store-bought ground beef, pork, or turkey.

Adding an assortment of different seasonings to different batches of your ground meat is an enjoyable way to experiment with flavorings in your ground meat and sausages. There is a multitude of seasonings available to choose from. My wife, Kate (author of several wild game cookbooks), recommends not seasoning the ground too heavily or it will overshadow the taste of the meat. She also suggests kneading the seasonings into the venison meat prior to cooking it. There is so much to say about the different seasonings that it could fill a book. The internet of course makes researching a subject so much easier. If seasonings are something you are interested in, search "seasonings for venison meat." Some seasonings that I have personal experience with for ground, sausage, and jerky are:

- GameButchers Shake & Rub Seasoning: www.gamebutcher.com
- cHarissa Spice Rub (wet and dry rubs): www.cHarissaspice.com
- Hi Mountain Seasonings: www.himtnjerky.com
- Hog Wild BBQ: www.hogwildbbq.com
- Bass Pro Shops' Mr. Steak: www.bassproshops.com
- Cookshack: www.cookshack.com
- Runnin' Wild Foods: www.runninwildfoods.com

I'd like to end with one important point. When it comes to grinders, an entry-level model is simply not designed to withstand more than casual use. They are made as appliances for homemakers who may intermittently grind small quantities of meat. If you use a machine like this to grind a lot of your deer meat, buy a fire extinguisher to place near the grinder.

Chapter 16

Stew Meat

This is a curtailed chapter because cutting up meat for stew is historically the stepchild compared to butchering all the other cuts on the deer (other than the ribs, which really get a lack of attention). An element about do-it-yourself home butchering, though, is to not forget about cutting venison

One of my favorite meals is a rib-sticking pot of venison stew. The savvy DIY butcher doesn't forget to cut up a sufficient amount of stew meat, including some meat from the finer cuts of venison. Often, stew meat is overlooked and is tossed into the ground meat bin. That is a big mistake.

for stew. A hearty batch of hot stew will warm your body and soul on a frigidly cold day in winter. It is genuinely the meal that can be said to have originated the saying "rib-sticking good." Frankly, I have never found a meal that beats a fulfilling bowl of a hearty, delicious, homemade venison stew. It keeps the mind, spirit, and inner person functioning at peak performance, particularly in winter.

Furthermore, venison stew provides an unending culinary enjoyment. A cook can create a wide-ranging variety of different types of homemade stews. These stews can be made with an extensive variety of ingredients, including onions, beans, peppers, tomatoes, corn, wheat kernels, celery, parsnip, cauliflower, winter squash, fennel, eggplant, swede, turnips, carrots, and more. If it is a vegetable, it can be added to any stew as a component. All types and colors of potatoes are also used in stews, along with a variety of barbeque-type sauces, different types of beers, wine, sherry, vodka, broths, a host of hot spicy sauces, and commercially made seasonings and flavorings. There is a lot of creative enjoyment to be had when making homemade stews from venison that you butchered yourself.

Unfortunately, many times the home butcher misses the opportunity, or doesn't take full advantage of cutting meat trimmings to be used for stew. The reason for this is an understandable one. Customarily, the meat is dedicated to making ground meat instead. As I stated in a prior chapter about making ground meat, it is the most versatile end result of all the meat you cut from the carcass. Therefore, it often dominates the attention of the home butcher more than any other cuts other than the backstraps and tenderloins. Consequently, the meat that can be set aside for stew is all too frequently overlooked.

When cutting up trim for stew, I usually cut pieces into half-inch cube-like portions that are perfectly fitting as bite size pieces. Because I enjoy stew so much, when it is time to package it Kate usually freezes about one-to two-pound portions or more in order to make a gigantic batch of stew when she prepares it. ("Petesie" likes a lot of venison meat in his stew *and* a lot of ground meat in his Italian meat sauce.)

Because stews are left to simmer for hours during their cooking, it is wise to make sure all the ingredients used in the stew, particularly all the veggies, are cut into bold chunks in order for them to hold up over the long cooking time. If they are small chunks, they will almost certainly become soupy pieces by time the stew is done. Another tip for slow cooking stews is to dredge the venison with seasoned flour before adding it in the stew.

Photo credit: Fiduccia Enterprises.

The meat I am cutting is destined to be used for stew. It contains meat from all parts of the deer, which will make the stew more flavorful.

Then it can be nicely browned in a skillet and tossed into the stew. This preparation will keep the meat holding together as it cooks, and it will also add a lot of flavor to the meat.

When cutting trim for stew meat, it is not necessary to use the tender cuts of the carcass. In fact, intentionally use the tougher cuts for stew meat instead. The long-term cooking process of homemade stews will turn even the toughest piece of meat into a tender morsel to be savored.

Photo credit: Fiduccia Enterprises.

I find the more venison meat used in a stew, the more enjoyable it is.

While it is cooking, it is also very important to not allow the stew to come to an active boil. By making sure this doesn't happen, you will prevent the meat from shrinking and getting tough and other ingredients from becoming mushy and tasteless. What any experienced chef, or home cook, strives to achieve when making stew is to have the stew simmer slowly enough not only to induce a continuously slow movement of the liquid and contents at the surface, but also to impart the enticing wisps of the wonderful odors of the stew emanating throughout the house or deer camp kitchen. Hopefully, by now I have helped you understand why you should absolutely not miss the opportunity to be sure to cut meat for stew when butchering your deer at home.

Chapter 17

Packaging, Freezing, and Thawing Venison

Freezer Wrapping Methods

There is no doubt that the very best way to package venison for long-term storage in a freezer is to vacuum seal the meat. With the latest technology, vacuum sealing devices have reached new heights of keeping venison air-tight and moisture-free. Air and moisture are the two most damaging elements to any type of long-term meat storage, wild game or domestic.

Additionally, vacuum sealing saves time by eliminating all the work associated with the formerly traditional process of paper wrapping venison with professional butcher-paper supplies and tape. For me, vacuum sealing venison, domestic meats, and a variety of other foods is the only method to store deer meat in the freezer without worrying about it going bad over a long period of time.

Vacuum sealing removes all the air from the vacuum bag, which causes the plastic to collapse around the food item's every contour. When oxygen is totally removed from a vacuum bag, the food item is literally sealed in a protected vacuum that eliminates the possibilities for the formation of ice crystals on the surface of the meat. The result is the meat is safely preserved for a far longer period of time in the freezer. Several research studies confirmed that meat items that have been vacuum sealed have a considerably long freezer storage life—up to three years. Within this time frame, most

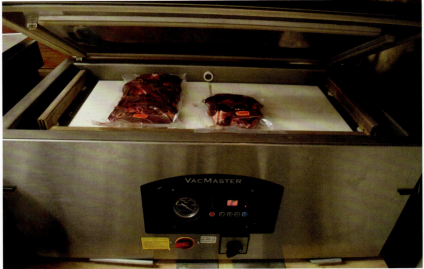

Photo credit: JB Person.

Since a vacuum seal will be protecting your hard-earned and valuable deer meat, it is wise to buy the best unit your budget can afford. Home models work well. But, if you plan on becoming a serious DIY butcher, a commercial unit like the one pictured here is more practical.

families will have consumed their venison bounty without worrying about freezer burn or loss of flavor and tenderness.

Prepared meals and liquids can also be vacuum sealed for a long period in the freezer. This can include a variety of different types of food items, in volumes large or small. For instance, this includes chilis, casseroles, stews, sauces, and all types of traditional meats, vegetables, and so on. For any do-it-yourself butcher, a vacuum sealer will prove itself to be among the most important tools in the lineup of butchering equipment.

At this juncture, I would like to take a short detour from this packaging topic to mention a piece of cooking equipment that uses vacuum-sealed food items. This cooking method, now commercially available for home cooks, takes your wild game (and domestic meats) to the next level. It is called a sous vide (pronounced sue veed).

Sous Vide

My wife, Kate, reminded me that I would be remiss if I didn't mention a cooking method that has long been used by professional chefs, but has only caught on among home chefs recently. It is a cooking technique that involves an appliance called a sous vide, which cooks vacuum-sealed venison, traditional meats, and most anything else with hot water.

As any caring spouse realizes, mentioning a spouse's credentials without regard to how many times they are talked about gains the other spouse unprecedented "good husband/wife points." Therefore, in a shameless attempt to gain more "good husband points," or if you happened to miss it earlier in the book, I will cite it again. Kate is a graduate of Cornell University's Hotel School. She has written several best-selling wild-game cookbooks, most published by Skyhorse Publishing (please buy one as I will gain even more good husband points if you do); and she is the director of operations at New York Custom Processing, LLC. Her high-end beef clientele includes Dole & Bailey, DeBragga and Spitler, Fleishers Craft Butchery, and White Gold Butchers. These businesses provide top-grade grass-fed and grain-finished beef to their clientele, which includes some of the nation's most recognized celebrity chefs. Equally important, Kate is also an accomplished big-game hunter.

Sous vide is a mouth-watering technique that Kate highly recommends as one that hunters should try, especially for preparing special prime cuts of venison such as tenderloins and backstraps. When cooking venison, or traditional meats like steak, with the sous vide method, you never have to be concerned about the doneness (color and texture) of the meat you are preparing. All you have to do, according to Kate, is place a seasoned (if you prefer) piece of meat and other food items that are vacuum sealed into a pot of water to the corresponding time and temperature desired. The end cooking result will be a perfectly done piece of meat every time.

As mentioned, this cooking technique is not new among professional chefs. They have been using it to serve perfectly done meats to their customers in the restaurants they own or work at for decades. Only lately has the sous vide process gained in popularity with home cooks. It has gained even more acceptance among hunters who prepare their wild game cuts of meat. The key advantages of cooking meat via the sous vide way is that it not only improves your favorite wild-game-meat dishes, it also cuts down on the lengthy time it takes to prepare and cook most dishes. It also eliminates the stress of cooking a venison or beef steak (or any other prime cut) to the desired doneness perfectly, virtually eliminating the possibilities of overcooking a venison tenderloin or backstrap. The downside to cooking with sous vide is that it may become an obsessive way of cooking not only wild and domestic meats but virtually everything, from crème brûlée to ribs and almost everything in between.

By now you may be wondering how this "sous vide" thing works and why the heck is it so much better than traditional cooking methods? Not to worry, I've been asked by Kate to tell you how it works

It is said that a sous vide will cook any vacuum-sealed meal to the same level as one prepared by an executive chef at a fine restaurant.

and why it is so much better than conventional cooking methods, particularly for wild game meats. According to Kate, when cooking with traditional methods, heat flows from a burner to a pan and then to the food. Or when food is prepared by cooking with the glowing elements found in an oven, the heat in the air surrounds the food, cooking it. The result is inevitable: The air in the oven and the metal in the pan become much hotter than the food requires and, therefore, the food item must be removed from the source of heat at just the right time or it ends up being overcooked. If, on the other hand, it is removed too early, you will be eating a bloody, undercooked piece of venison or beef.

When cooking meat with water, the temperature can be raised enough to get the food to the exact temperatures preferred and it can be removed exactly when it is done cooking (or it can even be left sitting in the water until it is ready to eat).

Instead, you can pour yourself a cold beer or a glass of dry red wine and relax and talk with your family or hunting buddies while your meal is cooking. This is another reason why sous vide is such a popular cooking method at camp or at home. It's failproof, it frees up the cook's time, and it improves the flavor, tenderness, and overall edibility of the wild game and domestic meats you cook. It will surely make you a legendary wild game chef. Enough said about sous vide? If not, Google it for more detailed information and where to buy this must-have piece of cooking equipment.

Paper Wrapping

For those who are storing venison without a vacuum sealer, the key element is to wrap the meat by focusing on locking in the meat moisture (for tenderness) while blocking out air, which can make the meat turn rancid and give it an off flavor. If you're going to use wrapping paper for freezing, it is critically important to use the best materials to keep your prized venison at its peak flavor. The bottom line here is the only way to do this is to *not* buy inexpensive wrapping supplies. This is only the first step in preserving your meat using this process, however.

When wrapping meat, focus your attention on eliminating air pockets around each cut. It's a good idea to use a quality heavy-duty cling-wrap for the first layer of wrapping. Again, concentrate on pressing this non-porous vapor barrier tightly to the cut of meat. The next step is to take an additional precaution by wrapping the meat a second time. This next covering should be with a quality-grade freezer wrapping paper. A good quality wrapping paper will have one side that is shiny and the other side dull. The glossy side should be placed against the meat. This freezer paper protects

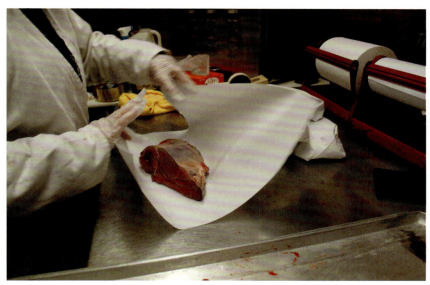

Photo credit: JB Person.

When freezing venison in paper, it is important to know how to avoid freezer burn or spoilage. Unlike plain butcher paper, freezer paper locks out air and locks in moisture because it's poly-coated on one side and the weight of the paper conforms closely to the shape of what you're wrapping.

the meat when it is in the freezer and when the meat comes in contact (or gets tossed around) with other stored frozen items. The inside of the paper (the shiny side) is actually plastic coated. This is the second and major moisture barrier that protects the meat from freezer burn, discoloration, loss of moisture, and eventually the possibility of becoming rancid.

Once you've completed wrapping each cut of meat, seal the wrapping paper with a quality masking tape. Don't be tempted to visit the dollar store and buy masking tape there. I can assure you you'll find better quality masking tapes elsewhere.

Another element that should also go without saying is the importance of labeling each package of venison. This one step, believe it or not, is often either totally overlooked or done without being thought through. When labeling packages of meat, you should always mark on the package with a waterproof pen in order to avoid the markings fading on the package. On each package, note the species, the cut of meat, the portion size (servings for one or more people), and, most important, the date the item was frozen. This recommendation also goes for anything that is vacuum sealed.

Getting back to packaging, freezing, and thawing meat properly, it isn't the latest news and/or rocket science for professionals in the food-processing and handling business that the old computer adage of "junk in, junk out" has meaning when it comes to freezing meat. Truth be told, the phrase is totally comparable to the quality of venison removed from being stored in a freezer. The fact is, meat simply isn't going to be any better than it was when it went into the freezer. When venison is incorrectly packaged with butcher paper or shrink-wrapped, it is destined to become freezer burned and, worse yet, go bad. It can also be left in the freezer past the recommended period of freezer time, which can also cause the meat to spoil.

Storing Venison Temporarily in a Refrigerator

After a deer is killed, many hunters traditionally will plan to prepare a meal at deer camp or at home, either the same day the animal was taken or, in most cases, within a couple of days. According to the United States Department of Agriculture (USDA), meat, including venison, can be kept unfrozen in a household refrigerator for a limited, safe period of time (see information in the sidebar).

Of course, this doesn't mean you can simply place a piece of venison on a dish, put it into the fridge, and expect it to retain its flavor and tenderness—even if it is left there for a day or so. Instead, it is as important to store venison properly in a home refrigerator as it is when storing it for a long-term period in a home freezer. The difference of storing meat in a refrigerator rather than a freezer is that it should be placed in the refrigerator unwrapped. The air in the refrigerator will help to dry out the surface of the meat slightly, which retains the flavor, tenderness, and condition of the meat. Kate

Photo credit: Fiduccia Enterprises.

If venison is going to be stored in the refrigerator for a short period of time before being eaten, make sure it is wrapped in a plastic bag.

simply puts the meat on a plate without covering it in order for it to dry out more quickly. Today, most refrigerators come with special enclosed compartments to safely store fresh meat that will inhibit odors and flavors from other foods in the fridge from escaping and, thereby, infusing your venison.

When preparing to freeze the packaged pieces of venison, it is a good idea to temporarily place them in the refrigerator first. This will bring down the temperature of the venison cuts. Once they have cooled down for four to six hours, place them in the freezer. The best way to do this is in batches. Place several cuts into the refrigerator; then add several cuts to the freezer. Don't overload the freezer all at once as this will raise the temperature of the freezer and it won't be able to freeze all the new pieces as quickly.

Quick Freezing Venison

Most all people have a combination refrigerator/freezer in their homes, but they are not the best choices for long-term storage of venison and even domestic meats. A much better choice for freezing your venison is a stand-up or chest freezer.

Freeze Venison Quickly

Freeze your packaged venison as fast as possible to maintain its quality. Rapid freezing, for all meats and other foods, prevents unwanted large ice crystals from forming throughout the product because the molecules don't have time to form into the characteristic six-sided snowflake. Slow freezing, conversely, creates large, disruptive ice crystals. During thawing, they damage the cells. This causes meat to "drip" and lose juiciness.

Many of Kate's customers request that their prime beef cuts be frozen rapidly on bread trays. The quick-freeze process helps retain the utmost quality of the cuts. This applies to venison as well. It's important to note that from the moment a deer is killed through all the processing in between,

These individual frozen packages have been quick frozen on the trays. This helps retain the flavor and quality of the meat.

Photo credit: Fiduccia Enterprises.

including the freezing and thawing processes, ill-treated venison is as inedible as stag caribou meat is during the peak rut. This is true no matter how many marinades, sauces, spices, and herbs are used to enhance its flavor.

Ideally, a food that's two inches thick should freeze completely in about two hours. If your home freezer has a "quick-freeze" shelf, use it. Never stack packages to be frozen. Instead, spread them out in one layer on various shelves, stacking them only after frozen solid.

To view the Food and Drug Administration's (FDA) Refrigerator & Freezer Storage Chart, go to the following link: (https://www.fda.gov/downloads/Food/ResourcesForYou/HealthEducators/ucm109315.pdf).

It should be noted that the FDA says because freezing 0°F (-18°C) keeps food safe indefinitely, the following recommended storage times are for *quality* only.

Fresh Meat (Venison, Beef, Veal, Lamb, and Pork)		
	Refrigerator	Freezer
Steaks	3 to 5 days	6 to 12 months
Chops	3 to 5 days	4 to 6 months
Roasts	3 to 5 days	4 to 12 months
Variety meats (tongue, kidneys, liver, heart, chitterlings)	1 to 2 days	3 to 4 months

Raw Hamburger, Ground and Stew Meat		
	Refrigerator	Freezer
Hamburger and stew meats	1 to 2 days	3 to 4 months
Ground turkey, venison, veal, pork, lamb	1 to 2 days	3 to 4 months

Does Freezing Destroy Bacteria and Parasites?

It's a mistake to believe that freezing meats (or other food items) will kill or destroy bacteria and parasites. The USDA advises that freezing to 0°F inactivates any microbes—bacteria, yeasts, and molds—present in food. Once thawed, however, these microbes can again become active, multiplying under the right conditions to levels that can lead to foodborne illness, caused by the bacteria salmonella or E. coli. Since they will then grow at about the same rate as microorganisms on fresh food, you must handle thawed items as you would any perishable food.

Trichina and other parasites can be destroyed by sub-zero freezing temperatures. However, very strict government-supervised conditions must be met. Home freezing cannot be relied upon to destroy trichina. Thorough cooking, however, will destroy all parasites.

Defrosting Venison

I can understand why the last topic in this chapter is one that may not be paid a lot of attention to because it seems so mundane or elementary to the reader. The fact is, if venison or traditional meats are defrosted incorrectly, it will affect the flavor, tenderness, and edibility of your prized game meat. In one of Kate's cookbooks, *The Venison Cookbook,* she recommends the safest and best way to thaw venison is by putting it into the refrigerator. Place the meat on a rack, in order to facilitate the excess blood to drain while the meat is defrosting. Depending upon the size of the piece of meat and the temperature setting of the refrigerator, thawing may take twelve hours to a day or even longer. In our home we keep a very cold refrigerator; in fact, it's so cold that ice crystals form in our containers of iced tea and orange juice. So, most of our venison needs more than a day to completely defrost. The second-best method for thawing frozen venison is under cool running water from the faucet. The cool running water will allow the frozen meat to warm up, yet not bring it up to a temperature where bacterial growth can begin. Thawing

Photo credit: Fiduccia Enterprises.

The best method for defrosting venison is in the refrigerator. Cover the meat with a damp cloth to minimize the moisture loss.

venison under running water will speed up the thawing process compared to thawing venison in the refrigerator, but sometimes this is impractical where running water may not be available, such as a remote hunting camp.

The last and least preferred method is to thaw venison and other traditional meats at room temperature. With venison, this can be a risky choice. Thawing meats at room temperature always permits bacterial growth at a surprisingly rapid rate. Bacteria love to multiply between temperatures of 45°F and 145°F. I don't think any kitchen falls outside of this range. Keeping venison below 45°F while defrosting will inhibit bacterial growth. The bacteria can still multiply, however, because the only way to kill most disease-causing bacteria is to subject them to temps above 170°F for a short period of time (about thirty seconds).

While bacterial growth will occur on the outside surfaces of tenderloins, backstraps, steaks, chops, and ribs, most bacteria is eliminated during cooking if the outside surfaces are seared or grilled at temps above 170°F. It is the ground meat and rolled roasts that are of the greatest concern. This is because the meat in the center of a package of ground venison has already been subject to air and possible contaminants, so it is highly susceptible to bacterial spoilage if left out at room temperature to thaw. This is of particular concern if the final cooking procedure does not bring the temperature of the meat to 170°F. This is the same, too, with a rolled roast. Roasts that have been rolled and tied prior to freezing have been subject to air and possible contaminants as well. If you follow the general guidelines of pulling a roast from the oven when it has reached an internal temperature of 125°F to 130°F, there may still be bacteria in the center of the roast. My universal recommendation, therefore, is to always thaw venison in the refrigerator, not at room temperature.

The question might be asked, why not thaw venison in the microwave? Kate experimented with this technique on occasion. She used small wrapped and unwrapped cuts, larger pieces under "lower" powers, smaller microwave ovens, and larger microwave ovens, and never found a happy solution to safely defrost venison in a microwave. The basis of microwave cooking is that the radiation generated by the oven penetrates the meat and agitates the water molecules. When the water molecules start moving around a lot, this generates heat which, in turn, thaws the meat. But, since most microwave radiation only reaches about two inches into the food, the heat can only reach further into the product after the outer portion is already much warmer. This is why most meats will brown on the outside yet remain raw on the inside when defrosted in the microwave. In addition, because venison is so lean, the meat fibers tend to shrink and lose moisture and, as a result, flavor. Venison can't afford to lose moisture. Even cuts like stew meat become tougher because the connective tissues and elastin shrink and become firmer. (Remember that stew meats must be cooked with moist heat methods to break down the connective tissue). While using a microwave to defrost venison may save time, it will cost you dearly in taste, quality, and edibility.

When meat is purchased at the supermarket, there is no way to know the condition or overall health of the animal. In addition, there's no way of knowing how it was processed, how the processed meat was handled, and how many different times it was handled before reaching the supermarket meat case. When dealing with our own game meat, we have total control over what happens to the meat prior to it becoming tablefare. By following proper field-care procedures and handling the meat meticulously throughout all steps from field dressing, skinning, quartering, butchering, wrapping, and freezing to thawing and cooking, you will ensure the venison meals you serve are as flavorful as any prime beef steak or tenderloin can possibly be.

Don't allow yourself to get into bad habits when it comes to defrosting venison or other meats. Nothing good ever results from mishandling venison. The bacteria from e. coli, salmonella, and similar parasites are nothing to fool around with. They can kill you.

Another interesting thing about venison is that once it has been completely cooked, it can be refrozen. This is because complete cooking transforms the cellular structure of the meat; it's almost like starting all over with fresh food.

Photo credit: Fiduccia Enterprises.

Hunters know exactly where their venison came from. Since all supermarkets sell quality USDA-inspected meat, knowing the details of where the meat came from is difficult to find out.

Take our household, for instance. Being of Italian descent, I love pasta; too much, I'm afraid, as I could eat it seven days a week. So Kate prepares a lot of her scrumptious and different types of meat sauces mostly with ground venison. Like Homer Simpson would say, "Mmmmm, ground venison." Since she makes more than we can eat in one sitting, the unused meat sauce gets frozen, as it is completely safe and okay to freeze it for future use. Likewise, other leftover venison cuts like stew meat from the neck, rump roasts, and so on can also be frozen and defrosted to use for stews or casseroles in the future. A last word on this the subject of defrosting is this: Trust the fact that properly defrosting your venison will noticeably retain its optimum taste, tenderness, and edibility.

Packaging, Freezing, and Thawing Venison Tips

- If you are not going to vacuum seal your venison, remember to try and remove as much air from any other packaging materials you are using.
- If using butcher paper to wrap and freeze your meat, go online and review any of several videos that show the proper step-by-step way to wrap venison, and what type of paper(s) to use.

Photo credit: Fiduccia Enterprises.

A very valuable tool for any DIY butcher is a quality vacuum-sealing machine. The wise DIY butcher knows that when it comes to buying an important piece of equipment like FoodSaver, the adage "You get what you pay for" applies.

- Freezer burn does not make food unsafe, merely dry in spots. It appears as grayish-brown leathery spots and is caused by air coming in contact with the surface of the food. Cut freezer-burned portions away before cooking the food.
- Heavily freezer-burned foods should be discarded for quality reasons.
- Sirloin tips, backstraps, and other prime choice boneless cuts of deer (and other big game) should not be steaked before freezing, as moisture escapes from each cut's surface. When that happens, smaller pieces lose more moisture than larger ones.
- When thawing venison in the refrigerator, the cool temperature minimizes bacterial growth.

Vacuum Sealers

Keep perishable foods safe from the harmful effects of airborne microorganisms with any of these three food vacuum sealers.

FoodSaver V3240

Users love watching the mostly automated FoodSaver V3240 vacuum sealer in action: Feed a bag into the slot, lower the handle, and the machine takes care of the rest. Its vertical construction saves counter space and makes the V3240 easier to store. A built-in cutter allows you to create custom-size bags.

Positive Features

- Inexpensive
- Built-in bag cutter
- Space-saving design
- Automatic operation

Need to Know

- Rather sturdy

Important Specs

Motor: 110 watts
Bag width: 11 inches
Bag price: $20 for 44 quarts
SMRP: Approx. $95

Weston 65-0501-W Professional Advantage Vacuum Sealer, 11-inch, Silver

For moderate use or sealing large, bulky packages of food, owners love the powerful suction and solid seal on the Weston Professional Advantage countertop vacuum sealer. Its fan-cooled motor won't overheat and an optional accessory hose lets you seal vacuum canisters too.

Positive Features

- Powerful, fan-cooled motor
- Intuitive controls
- Solid seal
- Good durability and customer service

Need to Know

- A wider sealing bar would be nice

Important Specs

Motor: 210 watts
Bag width: 11 inches
Bag price: $38 for 100 8x12 inches
SMRP: Approx. $180

VacMaster VP112S Chamber Vacuum Sealer

If you vacuum seal frequently or in large batches, or want to seal soup, marinades, or other messy foods, the VacMaster VP112S is a top pick. Owners love being able to adjust variables like vacuum speed, power, and the temperature of the heat sealer bar. The VP112S will also seal canning jars and vacuum canisters.

Positive Features

- Powerful
- Durable
- Versatile controls
- Handles liquids

Need to Know

- High-end price
- Heavy (46 pounds). Is designed for those who take self-sufficiency of foods to the next level.

Important Specs

Motor: 660 watts
Bag width: 12x14 inches
Bag price: $37 for 100 10x13 inches
SMRP: Approx. $480

Chapter 18

Venison Nutrition

As most of you reading this book already know, non-hunters are infamous for complaining about how venison has a strong, gamey flavor. The reason for that is because they are comparing the taste of venison to the flavor of farm-raised beef. As I have said in earlier chapters, the two meats are quite different. Domestic farm-raised, grain-finished beef is raised to be heavy (in weight) and to promote a substantial amount of cover fat (fat directly below the hide) and to have much more marbling (intramuscular fat).

Fat in beef provides that special zing of flavor. The reason a beef steer can accumulate so much fat is because a) it is fed a regimented diet designed to specifically put on as much weight on the animal as quickly as possible

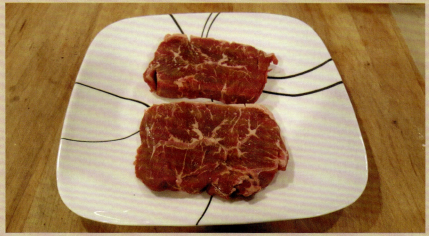

It's plain to see the marbling in these two beef steaks, which provides beef with its renowned flavor. If these were two pieces of wild venison, the marbling would be nearly impossible to see.

Photo credit: Fiduccia Enterprises.

before it is processed; b) scientific genetic advancements have accelerated the development of intramuscular fat (marbling) at an earlier stage in a steer's life; and c) steer are also much less active when compared to deer, and therefore gain and retain fat more easily.

In comparison, wild deer have very little intramuscular fat (marbling). The fat they do accumulate accounts for very little of the animal's overall weight. Venison is a lean meat because weight gain comes slowly, as nature doesn't require their weight to exceed a well-developed body. Deer are genetically geared to efficiently process the natural foods they consume throughout their lives (acorns, wild fruits, herbs, buds, twigs, grasses, legumes, etc.). All of the nourishment in these foods is converted into muscle. This is why venison can truly be said to be the original organic meat. While the fat marbling of beef provides its unique flavor when compared to the fat of venison, the comparison is like comparing apples to watermelons.

The fat of deer can cause a pungent flavor to the meat. Let's be clear here. Many times, the word "tallow" is referred to as deer fat. This is incorrect, or, at least, misused. Tallow is a rendered form of deer fat. Rendered means the fat has been cooked down and formed into a solid, yet pliable, substance. In this form, tallow can be used for candles, soaps, salves, and so on. In any form, deer fat is simply not flavorful and should be removed from your cuts of meat. The fat, along with the bones, should be removed before cooking to avoid the pasty taste they impart.

Deer fat has a higher melting point than beef fat. It also hardens faster when cooked venison cools down, resulting in

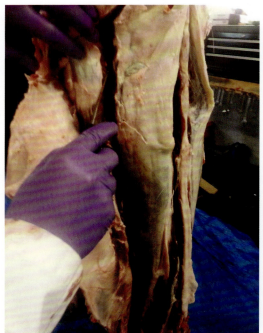

Photo credit: Fiduccia Enterprises.

When fat and tallow are left on the meat, they will produce a foul taste when cooked. It often leaves a pasty substance on the roof of one's mouth.

wax-like pieces that impart a foul flavor. Cooking deer bones will end up releasing deer fat, which will also cause the same bad flavor to whatever is being cooked along with it. A side note here is that venison does not have a long shelf life in the freezer, unless the fat and bone have been removed prior to freezing. Once venison fat and silverskin have been removed, the resulting meat will be lean and flavorful.

Despite what many non-hunters believe, or hunters who don't take care of their venison correctly from field to table, venison is a lean, dense meat that is a great addition to any healthy diet. It is lower in saturated fats and cholesterol when compared to beef or pork. Moreover, a three-ounce portion of venison has fewer calories than the same portion of chicken thighs.

Additionally, venison is lower in calories than some other domestic meats. For instance, a four-ounce portion of venison has about 180 calories. In contrast, a four-ounce portion of beef loin has 240 calories, while pork loin has 227 calories, and chicken thighs have 200 calories.

When it comes to high protein that doesn't contain saturated fat, a four-ounce portion of venison has twenty-six grams of protein with only three grams of fat (note I am not using the word tallow) and one gram of saturated fat. In comparison, a pork loin contains the same amount of protein, but, surprisingly, it has double the amount of total lipids and, unbelievably, *triple* the amount of saturated fat. Not surprisingly, beef has less protein and more fat than pork.

Consider vitamin B: a four-ounce portion of venison has 60 percent of the recommended daily allowance (RDA) of B12 and more than 20 percent of the RDA of B6, both of which help prevent homocysteine from accumulating in cells. Venison has 40 percent of the RDA of riboflavin (a.k.a. B2) and 30 percent of niacin (a.k.a. B3), which is important in energy production.

More important, as far as nutrition goes, there is no sodium, carbohydrates, sugar, or fiber in venison. A four-ounce portion of venison has an excellent source of iron with almost 30 percent of the RDA, as well as 25 percent of the RDA for phosphorus and 20 percent of the RDA for selenium and zinc. Most often venison meat does not contain any hormones or antibiotics.

When comparing venison to domestic meat, some professionals say venison contains less cholesterol than beef or pork. The fact is, depending on whose research you read, this may or may not be a misnomer. Most data from researchers, including from the USDA Agricultural Research Service and various health organizations, differ slightly. On the website cholesterol.org, their meat comparison chart states that a 3.5-ounce portion of venison has 158 milligrams of cholesterol and the same size portion of beef has 78 mg. Yet, in a 2017 article on LiveStrong.com by Joseph McAllister, he states, "A 3.5-ounce serving of venison steak—or 100 grams—contains 18 milligrams of dietary cholesterol. That is less than the cholesterol in most other meats, both red and white. Substituting venison for higher-cholesterol meats may be a beneficial health choice if you have excessively high levels of low-density lipoprotein cholesterol." In fact, cholesterol is more related to the lean meat of an animal rather than its fat. Contrary to popular belief, fat does not contain the most cholesterol.

Source: USDA National Nutrient Database for Standard Reference 28 slightly revised May 2016 Software v.3.8.6.4 2017-10-02					
Basic Report					
Report Run at: January 14	2018 14:59 EST				
Nutrient data for: 17164, Game meat, deer, raw					
Nutrient	Unit	1Value per 100 g	1 oz = 28.35g	1 lb = 453.6g	
Proximates					
Water	g	73.57	20.86	333.71	
Energy	kcal	120	34	544	
Protein	g	22.96	6.51	104.15	
Total lipid (fat)	g	2.42	0.69	10.98	
Carbohydrate, by difference	g	0	0	0	
Fiber, total dietary	g	0	0	0	
Sugars, total	g	0	0	0	
Minerals					
Calcium, Ca	mg	5	1	23	
Iron, Fe	mg	3.4	0.96	15.42	
Magnesium, Mg	mg	23	7	104	
Phosphorus, P	mg	202	57	916	
Potassium, K	mg	318	90	1442	
Sodium, Na	mg	51	14	231	
Zinc, Zn	mg	2.09	0.59	9.48	
Vitamins					
Vitamin C, total ascorbic acid	mg	0	0	0	
Thiamin	mg	0.22	0.062	0.998	
Riboflavin	mg	0.48	0.136	2.177	
Niacin	mg	6.37	1.806	28.894	
Vitamin B-6	mg	0.37	0.105	1.678	
Folate, DFE	µg	4	1	18	
Vitamin B-12	µg	6.31	1.79	28.62	
Vitamin A, RAE	µg	0	0	0	
Vitamin A, IU	IU	0	0	0	
Vitamin E (alpha-tocopherol)	mg	0.2	0.06	0.91	
Vitamin K (phylloquinone)	µg	1.1	0.3	5	
Lipids					
Fatty acids, total saturated	g	0.95	0.269	4.309	
Fatty acids, total monounsaturated	g	0.67	0.19	3.039	
Fatty acids, total polyunsaturated	g	0.47	0.133	2.132	
Cholesterol	mg	85	24	386	
Amino Acids					
Other					
Caffeine	mg	0	0	0	

Above is the nutritional data for game meat, raw, as analyzed by the USDA. Use this chart to compare the nutritional aspects of deer with other types of meat.

There are some cuts of venison that are slightly lower in cholesterol than pork or beef, like the round steak or roast. But, believe it or not, venison contains a slightly higher average level of cholesterol than comparable domestic meats. See the nutritional chart from the USDA National Nutrient Database for Standard Reference for the nutrient values of venison loin.

This chart is specific to raw meat of deer. There is a host of detailed nutritional facts, figures, and charts that you can access via the USDA's web site (http://ndb.nal.usda.gov). Some of the charts are on venison cuts, including but not limited to deer meat cooked, deer meat raw and cooked, deer meat tenderloin cooked, deer meat top round one-inch steak cooked, and so on.

Chapter 19

Delicious Venison Recipes

The culmination of all your work, from the instant you field dress your deer to the moment you place a mouth-watering dish of venison on the table before friends and family, is well worth the effort. Seeing the looks on everyone's faces as they enjoy what you have cooked is always gratifying. But more important, you know all the work you went through to bring the most tender and flavorful meat from field to table was worth the effort. All these factors make DIY butchering enjoyable. It also provides a sense of pride to the hunter who stalked, killed, took care of, and prepared the wild game.

Below are some of the most scrumptious venison recipes we have enjoyed at home. I am especially lucky that even though I enjoy cooking venison, Kate's skills as a wild-game cook are unsurpassed. These dishes, other than the rouladen, were created and prepared by Kate.

Rinsrouladen is more commonly referred to as rouladen. It is also known as beef olive in other parts of Europe. The word roulade means "to roll," and rouladen is exactly that, a roll of venison meat that is stuffed with other fixings and cooked by braising and simmering all the ingredients. It is one of my favorite ways to prepare venison, be it deer, moose, elk, or caribou.

Rouladen is an old German meat dish. It traditionally includes bacon, onions, whole grain brown mustard, and dill pickles that are wrapped in *thinly* sliced pieces of beef, which is then cooked. In the traditional German beef dish, the recipe also includes carrots, mushrooms, potatoes, and other root vegetables.

The most popular cut for rouladen comes from the roasts. For those who prefer more tender cuts, the backstraps will take this dish to the next level! The fact is, however, that this traditional old-world German recipe can be made with just about any cut of venison. By simply pounding the cuts very thin and then cooking them via a long, slow braise, you'll be able to cut the meat with a fork.

Photo credit: Peanut butterinmyhair.com

Any thick cut of venison that doesn't have a lot of connective tissue makes an ideal cut for rouladen.

Photo credit: Fiduccia Enterprises.

These thin, long cuts of venison will work well for either a rouladen recipe or a cutlet recipe. To get the best results, pound the pieces thin for uniform thickness.

Photo credit: Fiduccia Enterprises.

When you serve this dish to family and friends, you not only enhance your cooking reputation, but also cement the reason why we hunt.

To make the job easier, it is helpful to butterfly the cuts of roast using a sharp knife. Kate likes to ensure that once she pounds any piece of meat flat using a meat mallet, she finishes it off by using a "Jaccard" tenderizer tool. This technique will make any piece of meat so tender it can be cut with a fork. For this recipe, try to get the cuts to an overall thickness of about one eighth of an inch or so. An ideal size for a roulade would be at least four by six inches or so.

Venison Rouladen

Yield: 2 to 3 servings
Prep Time: 30 minutes
Cook Time: 1 hour 45 minutes

Ingredients

2 lbs. venison roast, sliced and pounded as thinly as possible
½ to ¾ cup (to taste) German whole-grain mustard (or brown mustard)
Sea salt (or kosher salt) and freshly ground pepper
Dill pickles, quartered lengthwise
1 small and/or medium onion, thinly sliced
2 slices bacon per piece, partially cooked and cut in half
3 tablespoons flour + more for dredging meat
3 tablespoons oil (preferably canola)
3 tablespoons unsalted butter
1 can (14 oz.) beef stock
⅓ cup dry red wine
1 tablespoon cornstarch mixed with ½ cup water to thicken gravy, if needed
3 cloves garlic, sliced thinly
2 tablespoons chopped parsley (as an optional garnish)
1 small box of toothpicks for fastening

Preparation

Customarily, the venison is smeared with whole-grain mustard, but any mustard of your choice can be used. Coat each piece with about 1 tablespoon of mustard, spreading it evenly over the surface of each thinly pounded piece of meat. Season the meat with sea salt and pepper. Place the dill pickles slices (again, use pickles of choice) near one end of the flattened meat and then layer on the thinly sliced onions, and two pieces of bacon. From the near side, roll the venison sheet of meat up tightly to ensure the stuffing ingredients remain within the center. Secure the rolls firmly using toothpicks. Next, roll each piece so that they are evenly coated in the all-purpose flour and set aside.

Now pre-heat three tablespoons of oil. Using a skillet or other type pan that can be covered with an accompanying lid, set the temperature to a medium-high heat. Once the oil is hot, place the venison rolls into the skillet and brown them, flipping occasionally to cover all sides. How thinly the meat is pounded will be the determining factor of how long you should sear the rolls on all sides. Very thinly sliced pieces shouldn't be cooked more than 45 seconds on each side and thicker slices not more than a minute or two on each side.

Once the meat is browned, remove it from the pan and set it aside. Pour out any leftover oil. Add 3 tablespoons of butter to the pan. Once melted, add three tablespoons of the flour to the melted butter. With a watchful eye, stir the flour well into the butter until the flour becomes lightly browned. Now it's time to add the beef broth and dry red wine to the pan while scraping any stuck-on bits from the bottom of the pan into the mix. Bring the liquid to a boil and then place the venison rolls back into the pan. With a tight-fitting lid, cover the pan and immediately reduce the temperature to a setting of low heat for about 1½ hours. The low temperature will allow the rouladen to just simmer/braise during that time. It is important to keep a keen eye on the rouladen while cooking this recipe as the rolls need to be flipped halfway through the cooking process. After about 30 to 45 minutes, check the doneness of the rolls. Once the rouladen is cooked, remove them from the pan.

If the gravy needs to be thickened, turn the heat back up to medium-high. Mix an additional tablespoon of corn starch into ½ cup of water and stir the mixture briskly into the existing gravy. The gravy should be boiled and stirred until it is thick enough to coat the back of a spoon.

When serving roulade, slice the rolls into medallions and liberally coat each piece in the gravy. Dish up over mashed potatoes, roasted root vegetables, or the traditional German boiled potatoes and dumplings. Add parsley to serve.

Following are several of my favorite venison recipes from Kate. They are all specifically designed to be easy to prepare and scrumptious. I am sure that they will be a hit at deer camp or at home with your family. They have even been known to convert hard-core non-eaters-of-venison into venison lovers. Enjoy or, as we say in Italian, "Mangia!"

Kate's "Hoochie Mamma" Chili

Bar none, if you enjoy spicy food, Hoochie Mamma is the first recipe you'll want to prepare. On an ice-cold winter's day, it'll warm the soul and on a hot summer's day it'll exhilarate the tongue—either way, it's sure to ring your bell.

Photo credit: Fiduccia Enterprises.

Yield: 8 servings
Prep Time: 15 minutes
Cooking Time: 2 hours

Ingredients

2 lbs. ground venison
2 medium onions, chopped
1 green bell pepper, chopped
3 cloves garlic, minced
1 can (28 oz.) whole tomatoes, undrained
1 can (15 oz.) tomato sauce
1½ cups water
⅓ cup sliced serrano peppers or jalapeño or habanero peppers, depending upon your tolerance for hot and spicy food
¼ cup chili powder
1 tablespoon cayenne pepper
1 tablespoon cumin
½ teaspoon salt
½ teaspoon black pepper
1 bay leaf
1 can (15 oz.) kidney beans, drained
Corn bread or rolls for accompaniment, optional

Preparation

In large Dutch oven, cook venison, onion, green pepper, and garlic over medium heat until venison is no longer pink and vegetables have softened, stirring occasionally to break up meat. Add tomatoes, tomato sauce, water, serrano peppers, chili powder, cayenne pepper, cumin, salt, black pepper, and bay leaf. Heat to boiling, then reduce heat and simmer, uncovered, for about 1½ hours, stirring occasionally. Add kidney beans and simmer for about 30 minutes longer. Remove bay leaf. Serve chili with corn bread or fresh baked rolls. A cool drink would be nice too!

Sloppy Does

Much like chili that can cook on low heat all day in the crockpot, so does this recipe for Sloppy Does. It can also be prepared in less than an hour on the stovetop if time is short.

Yield: 8 sandwiches
Prep Time: 15 minutes
Cook Time: 8 hours, slow cooking

Ingredients

1½ lbs. ground venison
1 cup onion, chopped
3 cloves garlic, minced
1 cup chili sauce
½ cup green pepper, chopped
¼ cup celery, chopped
½ cup chopped mushrooms
¼ cup water
2 tablespoons light brown sugar
2 tablespoons prepared mustard
2 tablespoons red wine vinegar
2 tablespoons Worcestershire sauce
2 teaspoons chili powder
8 hamburger buns, split

Preparation

In a large skillet over medium heat, cook the venison, onion, and garlic until the meat is browned. While that is cooking, in a slow-cooker or crock pot, combine the remaining ingredients, except for the buns. Stir to mix well. Add in the meat mixture when it is done and mix thoroughly. Cover and cook on low for 6 to 8 hours. If the mixture is too watery, take the lid off for the last hour or so to thicken it up.

Lightly toast or grill the buns and spoon the mixture over them.

Venison Tamale Pie

Here's a dish that takes a little bit of extra time because of the cornmeal crust. But it's worth the effort! It was during a whitetail hunting trip to south Texas that we first tasted true tamales. We were hunting at the Lazy Fork Ranch and the cook prepared many dishes native to her Mexican homeland. Although Kate wasn't able to get the exact recipe from her, this one comes close—and she hasn't had any complaints on the receiving end when it's served!

Yield: 6 servings
Prep Time: 20 minutes
Cooking Time: 40 minutes

Ingredients

Filling
1 tablespoon canola oil
1 lb. ground venison
4 scallions, chopped
1 can (8 oz.) tomato sauce
1 cup whole-kernel corn, drained
¼ cup chopped Anaheim peppers (for more zing, use a blend of Anaheim and jalapeño peppers)
¼ cup cornmeal
1 teaspoon chili powder
1 teaspoon salt
½ teaspoon pepper
½ teaspoon cumin
¼ teaspoon crumbled dried oregano leaves

Cornmeal Pie Crust

1 cup all-purpose flour, plus additional for rolling out crust
2 tablespoons cornmeal
⅓ cup vegetable shortening
3 to 4 tablespoons cold water

Topping

1 egg, lightly beaten
¼ cup evaporated milk
½ teaspoon dry mustard
1 cup shredded Monterey Jack cheese
1 cup shredded cheddar cheese
6 pitted black olives, sliced
Sour cream and chopped tomatoes for garnish, optional

Preparation

Heat oven to 425°F.

In large skillet, heat oil over medium heat. Add venison and cook until no longer pink, stirring to break up. Drain. Mix in remaining filling ingredients. Let simmer for 5 minutes, then remove from heat.

In small bowl, blend together flour and cornmeal. Cut in shortening with pastry blender or two knives. When mixture resembles coarse meal or very small peas, add water a little at a time, mixing with fork until dough is formed. Roll out pastry on a floured surface until it forms a 10-inch circle. Fit the pasty into a 9-inch deep-dish pie pan and crimp the edges.

Spoon filling into pie crust. Place pie pan on baking sheet and bake for 25 minutes. While it is baking, prepare the topping for the pie. Combine egg, milk, and mustard in medium bowl; mix well. When pie has baked for 25 minutes, remove from oven, sprinkle cheeses over filling, and pour milk mixture on top. Decorate with sliced olives. Return to oven and bake for an additional 5 to 7 minutes. Let stand for 10 minutes before serving. Serve with sour cream and chopped tomatoes.

Asian Venison Lettuce Wraps

Here is a tasty and quick way to prepare ground venison as an appetizer.

Yield: 3 to 4 servings as an appetizer
Prep Time: 15 minutes
Cook Time: 15 minutes

Ingredients

1 tablespoon + 2 tablespoons sesame oil, divided
1½ lbs. ground venison
1 teaspoon garlic powder
1 cup mushrooms, minced
1 cup (8 oz.) water chestnuts, minced
¼ cup onions, minced
2 tablespoons hoisin sauce
¼ cup of your favorite teriyaki-type sauce
Lettuce leaves
Chinese mustard

Preparation

Heat a large sauté pan over medium heat. Add 1 tablespoon sesame oil to warm slightly. Add in the ground venison and cook until it is no longer pink. While it is cooking, sprinkle with garlic powder. When the meat is browned, remove it from the pan. Do not drain. Let it cool slightly.

Combine the cooked venison, mushrooms, water chestnuts, and minced onions in a bowl. Return empty pan to medium heat. Add 2 tablespoons sesame oil and add in venison mixture. Season with hoisin sauce and teriyaki sauce. Mix well to let all flavors blend together. Serve in lettuce leaves and top each portion with a bit of Chinese mustard.

Roast Mustard Loin of Venison

Yield: 8 to 12 servings
Prep Time: 10 minutes
Marinating Time: 1 to 2 hours
Cooking Time: 30 minutes

Ingredients

4 to 5 lbs. venison loin, well-trimmed (you may also use 2 smaller portions)
2 to 3 cups Simple Marinade (at the end of this chapter)
1 tablespoon + ¼ cup olive oil, divided
1 cup Dijon mustard
⅓ cup chopped scallions
⅓ cup dry white wine
¼ cup bread crumbs
4 large cloves garlic, minced
1 teaspoon sea salt
½ teaspoon crumbled dry sage
½ teaspoon crumbled dried thyme
¼ teaspoon pepper

Preparation

Measure venison loin against a large skillet and cut into halves if necessary to fit skillet. Place venison in a non-aluminum pan and pour the marinade over, turning to coat. Cover and refrigerate 1 to 2 hours, turning occasionally. Remove venison from marinade and pat dry; discard marinade.

Heat oven to 375°F. In large skillet, heat 1 tablespoon of the oil over high heat until it is hot but not smoking. Add venison and quickly sear on all sides. Transfer venison to roasting pan; set aside.

In blender or food processor, combine remaining ¼ cup oil with the mustard, scallions, white wine, bread crumbs, garlic, salt, sage, thyme, and pepper. Process until smooth; the coating should be thick. Spread coating evenly over the venison. Roast to desired doneness, 15 to 17 minutes for medium-rare. Remove venison from oven when internal temperature is 5°F less than desired. Tent meat with foil and let rest for 10 to 15 minutes before slicing.

Sesame Venison Medallions

Blended sesame oil combines the pale-yellow sesame oil that has no smell and is often used for frying with the dark brown Chinese sesame oil that has a strong, nutty taste. The combination is excellent, especially when used in a marinade, as in this recipe.

Serves: 6 to 8
Prep Time: 10 minutes
Marinating Time: 1 to 2 hours
Cook Time: 5 minutes

Ingredients

¼ cup canola oil
¼ cup blended sesame oil
¼ cup soy sauce
2 tablespoons fresh lemon juice
2 tablespoons grated fresh ginger
1½ to 2 lbs. venison loin, cut into medallions about ½- to ¾-inch thick
2 tablespoons sesame seeds

Preparation

In a small non-metallic bowl, whisk together the oils, soy sauce, lemon juice, and ginger. Place the venison medallions in a shallow glass baking dish. Pour the marinade over the medallions. Turn to coat completely. Cover the dish with plastic wrap and let it sit in the refrigerator for 1 to 2 hours.

Remove the medallions from the refrigerator and let come to room temperature.

Preheat the grill for about 20 minutes. The grill should be hot enough so that you can hold your hand over it for only a few seconds.

Remove the medallions from the marinade and pat dry. The leftover marinade can be placed in a small saucepan, boiled, and then used as a baste if desired.

Lightly oil the grill plate. Place the medallions on the grill and let cook 2 to 3 minutes each side. Do not cook more than medium rare. Remove the medallions and set aside for 5 minutes for the juices to set.

In a small skillet over medium heat, place the sesame seeds. Let the seeds cook to a light golden-brown color. Shake the pan occasionally to move the seeds around. Remove them from the heat and sprinkle on the medallions. Serve the medallions immediately.

Venison Filet with Morels

Every time I take any big-game animal (especially a whitetail), I take care when I remove the backstraps. Even though I have been doing this for years, I find that each time I am removing the back-straps, I am always planning in my head how I will cook this choicest of all cuts. One way to enhance backstraps to their max is with this recipe!

Servings: 3 to 4
Prep Time: 15 minutes
Cooking Time: Under 30 minutes

Ingredients

1 cup (2 sticks) butter, divided in half
2 tablespoons pepper
1 to 2 lbs. venison backstrap or tenderloin, cut into ½-inch-thick medallions
½ cup + 2 teaspoons all-purpose flour, divided
8 oz. fresh morel mushrooms, chopped
⅓ cup sherry
2 tablespoons freshly chopped chives or wild onion tops
⅓ cup beef broth
Salt and pepper

Preparation

In Dutch oven, heat one stick of the butter over medium-high heat until sizzling. Press the pepper into the loin steaks and then dip them into the ½ cup flour. Add to hot butter and sauté until just browned on both sides. Take care not to overcook the venison. Remove from Dutch oven and keep warm.

Add remaining butter, mushrooms, sherry, and chives to Dutch oven. Cook for 5 to 7 minutes, or until morels are tender. Meanwhile, combine remaining 2 teaspoons flour and beef broth in small bowl, stirring to blend and remove any lumps. When mushrooms are tender, add broth mixture, stirring constantly. Cook, stirring constantly, until sauce thickens. Season sauce with salt and pepper to taste. Divide venison steaks between plates and top with mushroom sauce.

Garlic-Lime Venison Steak

This is one that was derived from a recipe that was shared with me by Kate's college friend, Sylvia. Sylvia was from Cuba and loved to share with us some of her native recipes during the seemingly endless winter months in upstate New York. I later adapted this flavorful one for venison.

Yield: 4 servings
Prep Time: 15 minutes
Cooking Time: 10 minutes

Ingredients

Garlic-Lime Rub

1 teaspoon kosher salt
½ teaspoon freshly ground black pepper
6 cloves garlic, minced
½ teaspoon cumin
⅛ teaspoon cayenne pepper
½ cup fresh lime juice
2 tablespoons olive oil

Steaks

4 venison steaks, trimmed of all connective tissue and fat, 6 to 8 oz. each
1 lb. portobello mushrooms, sliced ¼-inch thick
2 tablespoons olive oil
Salt to taste
Pepper to taste

Preparation

Make the garlic-lime rub. In a mortar, combine the salt, pepper, garlic, cumin, and cayenne pepper. Grind the ingredients to a paste. Slowly drizzle in the lime juice and olive oil, alternating, until it has reached a smooth consistency.

Place the venison steaks in a glass baking dish and, with a pastry brush, lightly coat both sides of the steaks with the garlic-lime rub. Let sit for 15 to 20 minutes.

While the steaks sit, preheat the grill for about 20 minutes. The grill should be hot enough so you can hold your hand over it for only a few seconds.

Place the mushrooms in a bowl and drizzle with olive oil and a little salt. Toss to coat. Place the mushrooms in an oiled, long-handled, hinged grill basket. Set on the grill to cook in a cooler section of the grill.

Place the steaks in the center of the grill. Grill about 2 minutes each side, while basting with the rub. Grill the mushrooms about 2 to 3 minutes per side, seasoning with salt and pepper.

Transfer the steaks to plates, and let sit for a few minutes. Serve with the grilled mushrooms on the side.

Venison Stew With Barley

Since this stew is prepared in a skillet, make sure you have one that's large enough—at least 12 inches in diameter. The aroma while this stew is cooking will have you fighting back hungry ones until it's time to eat!

Yield: 4 servings
Prep Time: 30 minutes
Cooking Time: 2 hours

Ingredients

½ lb. pearl onions*
9 large fresh shiitake mushrooms, stems removed and discarded (½ to ¾ lb. white mushrooms may be substituted)
2 cups peeled, cubed butternut squash (1-inch cubes)
1 tablespoon canola oil
1 teaspoon + ¼ teaspoon crumbled dried thyme, divided
1½ lbs. boneless venison shoulder or rump, cut into 1-inch cubes
Seasoned pepper (such as McCormick California Style Garlic Pepper)
3 cups beef stock or canned unsalted beef broth
1 bay leaf
1 large clove garlic, minced
¾ cup pearl barley
Water as needed (approx. ¾ cup)
Chopped fresh parsley for garnish

*You can use thawed frozen pearl onions in place of fresh if you'd like; it'll save you some time, as you won't need to boil and peel them.

Preparation

Heat large saucepan of water to boiling. Add pearl onions and boil for 2 to 3 minutes to loosen skins. Drain and cool slightly. Cut off root ends. Squeeze onions from stem end; the onions will slip out of their skins. Place onions in large bowl.

Cut mushroom caps into halves (white mushrooms may be halved or left whole, depending on size). Add mushrooms, squash, oil, and 1 teaspoon of the thyme to the bowl with onions, stirring gently to coat vegetables. Heat large nonstick skillet over high heat. Add vegetables and sauté until browned. Use slotted spoon to return vegetables to bowl; set aside.

Sprinkle venison with seasoned pepper. Brown seasoned venison cubes in small batches and transfer to a plate. When all venison is browned, return to skillet. Add beef stock, bay leaf, garlic, and remaining ¼ teaspoon thyme. Heat to boiling. Reduce heat, cover, and simmer for 15 minutes. Stir in barley. Cover and simmer for 45 minutes. Stir vegetables into stew. Cover and simmer until vegetables and barley are tender, about 45 minutes longer; add water as needed during cooking to keep mixture moist. Remove bay leaf. Sprinkle stew with parsley and serve.

Rainy Day Venison Chili

There's nothing that remains more embraced by campers or folks at the cabin than a bowl of hot steaming chili during hunting season. You can't go wrong with this one.

Yield: 4 servings
Prep Time: 15 to 20 minutes
Cooking Time: 1½ hours

Ingredients

4 slices bacon, chopped
1 cup chopped onion
¼ cup chopped green pepper
1 lb. venison, cut in ½- to 1-inch cubes

1 can (15 oz.) kidney beans, drained
1 can (11 oz.) whole-kernel corn, drained
1 cup chopped fresh or canned tomatoes (if canned, drain before chopping)
1 cup chopped mushrooms (either fresh or canned)
2 teaspoons chili powder
1 teaspoon cumin
½ teaspoon salt
3 cloves garlic, minced
1 cup water
¼ cup flour

Preparation

In a Dutch oven, cook bacon over medium heat until just crisp, stirring occasionally. Add onion and green pepper to Dutch oven; cook until tender, stirring occasionally. Remove the bacon, pepper, and onion from the Dutch oven and set aside. Add venison and cook until meat is browned on all sides, stirring occasionally. While venison is cooking, in a medium bowl combine the remaining ingredients except the flour; toss well to combine. When venison is browned, return the bacon, onions, green peppers to the Dutch oven, then add the other mixture. Stir well to mix thoroughly. Set lid on top and let simmer for 45 minutes to 1 hour. Sprinkle a little flour in to thicken the chili as needed.

Venison Vegetable Frittata

Frittatas are ideal dishes for spring and summer because they're light and they cook quickly. I tasted my first frittata at a Mama Lucci's restaurant in the Little Italy section of New York City many years ago. It was a hot summer's day, and the lunchtime crowd had packed the air-conditioned bistros. Kate and  I decided to take a sidewalk seat instead and do the "New York" thing—people watching while enjoying a light meal.

This dish is perfect when we've had an early rise to start working in the yard and have skipped a good breakfast. Serve it with a side of salsa and fresh-baked biscuits.

Yield: 6 servings
Prep Time: 15 minutes
Cooking Time: 30 minutes

Ingredients

½ lb. ground venison
Salt, black pepper, and cayenne pepper
¼ cup unsalted butter, divided equally
3 tablespoons minced shallots
1 tablespoon minced garlic
1 lb. fresh button mushrooms, sliced
½ cup diced fresh zucchini
8 eggs, room temperature
½ lb. fresh spinach leaves, torn or finely chopped
1 cup small-curd cottage cheese
¼ cup grated Parmesan cheese
1 tablespoon olive oil

Preparation

Cook venison in large skillet over medium heat until no longer pink, stirring to break up. Season to taste with salt, black pepper, and cayenne pepper; set aside.

In large omelet pan (minimum 12 inches), melt 2 tablespoons of the butter over medium heat. Add shallots and garlic and cook for about 3 minutes. Add mushrooms and zucchini. Sauté until liquid from the mushrooms has evaporated. Remove from heat and set aside to cool.

Heat broiler. Beat eggs in large bowl. Mix spinach, cottage cheese, and cooled venison mixture. Add the cooled mushroom mixture and stir until well combined.

Set omelet pan over medium-high heat. Melt remaining 2 tablespoons butter. Add egg mixture; as it begins to set, shake the pan to ensure it does not stick. Turn heat to low. Without stirring, continue cooking for about 10 minutes, checking to make sure the eggs do not stick to the pan.

When egg mixture is almost completely set, sprinkle Parmesan cheese and drizzle oil on top of the frittata. Place pan under the broiler to melt cheese; be careful not to overcook. Slide frittata onto serving platter; cut into 6 portions.

Santa Fe Venison Chili

Chipotle peppers are ripe jalapeño chiles that have been dried and then smoked. They are found canned with red tomato sauce in most ethnic sections of grocery stores.

Yield: 4 to 6 servings
Prep Time: 25 minutes
Cooking Time: 1½ hours

Ingredients

½ cup canola oil
2 lbs. venison, trimmed free of all fat and connective tissue, chopped
8 cloves garlic, minced
1 onion, chopped
2 tablespoons chipotle peppers in adobo sauce
5 medium tomatoes, seeded and chopped
1 teaspoon ground cumin
1 tablespoon Mexican oregano
2 cups water
2 cups beef stock
Salt and freshly ground pepper to taste

Preparation

Heat the oil in a Dutch oven over medium-high heat. Add in the venison, garlic, and onion. Stir frequently to avoid meat lumping together (cook in batches if your pan is not large enough). Cook until meat has browned, about 10 minutes. Add the chipotle puree, tomatoes, cumin, oregano, water, and beef stock. Bring to a simmer, uncovered, and let cook for about 1 to 1½ hours, stirring occasionally. Season with salt and pepper to taste. Serve hot with accompaniments of sour cream, grated cheddar cheese, corn bread, and butter.

Fast And Easy Teriyaki Jerky

Yield: 1 to 1½ pounds of dry jerky
Prep Time: 15 minutes
Marinating Time: 8 to 12 hours
Drying Time for Oven: 4 to 6 hours
Drying Time for Electric Dehydrator: 5 hours

Ingredients

5 lbs. venison, preferably a sirloin or round cut
6 oz. teriyaki sauce
4 oz. soy sauce
2 teaspoons black pepper

Preparation

Rinse meat thoroughly in cold water to remove any remaining hair, blood, or other foreign matter. Trim all fat, tallow, and silverskin completely from the meat. Slice meat into ¼- to ½-inch-thick strips across the grain.

Photo credit: Fiduccia Enterprises.

Photo credit: Fiduccia Enterprises.

Photo credit: Fiduccia Enterprises.

Photo credit: Fiduccia Enterprises.

Place all ingredients except the meat in a sturdy zip-top plastic bag. Close bag. Hold bag securely at the top, shake vigorously to mix ingredients well. Open bag, add meat, and shake vigorously until the meat is well covered. Allow to marinate in refrigerator for 8 to 12 hours, turning bag frequently.

Drain meat well in a strainer. Discard marinade. DO NOT REUSE. Blot the meat strips dry on paper towels.

Place meat on dehydrator trays or oven racks, making sure not to allow the strips of meat to touch.

Allow the strips to dry in the oven (150°F to 200°F with oven door slightly ajar) or in an electric dehydrator (145°F). When the jerky is done, it will crack but not break when bent.

Simple Marinade

Great for loin cuts, steaks, and roasts. Cover and refrigerate 1 to 3 hours.

Yield: 1¼ cups
Prep Time: 5 minutes

Ingredients

1 cup olive oil
3 tablespoons lemon juice
1 tablespoon chopped garlic
1 tablespoon crushed black peppercorns
Crumbled dried oregano to taste

Preparation

Combine all ingredients in a nonreactive container. Keep chilled until used.

Photo credit: Fiduccia Enterprises.

Tri-Color Peppercorn Rub

Kate's thought on adding flavor to the quality cuts of venison is . . . less is more! The peppercorns in this simple rub complement the taste of venison nicely. As they cook over high heat, the peppercorns caramelize and sear into the outer layer of the meat, helping to lock in the juices. This rub works well with grilled or seared sirloin steaks and loin medallions. Let rub sit on the meat a good 6 to 8 hours.

Yield: Over ⅔ cup
Prep Time: 5 minutes

Ingredients

3 tablespoons whole black peppercorns
3 tablespoons whole white peppercorns
3 tablespoons whole pink peppercorns
1 tablespoon mustard seed
2 teaspoons garlic powder
1½ teaspoons kosher salt

Preparation

Combine all ingredients in a spice mill and process to a coarse powder, or grind coarsely with a mortar and pestle.

Photo credit: Liesa Cole.

Mustard Sauce

This is a great dipping sauce with fondues and can also be served as an accompaniment for grilled venison steaks.

Yield: 1 cup
Prep Time: 5 minutes

Ingredients

⅔ cup sour cream or yogurt
3 tablespoons mayonnaise
1 tablespoon Dijon mustard
Salt and white pepper to taste

Preparation

In a small bowl, combine all ingredients. Stir well and serve.

Chapter 20

Toxoplasmosis: What You Should Know

———

Throughout this book I often recommended cooking venison to a rare to medium-rare state. In many other wild game cookbooks, the recommendations are always to cook venison on the rare side, especially the tender cuts. But it would be remiss of me not to mention a potential health complication related to a parasite that both feral and domestic cats can carry and which can be transmitted to deer. Once a deer is infected with this parasite, it can be transmitted to humans by eating *undercooked* venison.

What is toxoplasmosis?

According to the Center for Disease Control (CDC), *Toxoplasma gondii* is a single-celled parasite that causes a disease known as toxoplasmosis. Toxoplasmosis is found worldwide. In the United States, more than 60 million people may be infected with the *Toxoplasma* parasite. Of those who are infected, very few have symptoms because a healthy person's immune system usually keeps the parasite from causing illness. However, pregnant women and individuals who have compromised immune systems should be cautious; for them, a *Toxoplasma* infection could cause serious health problems.

A study in 2015 in the journal *EcoHealth* connected white-tailed deer and free-roaming feral cats to the disease toxoplasmosis. Lead author Gregory Ballash, Ohio State University's Department of Veterinary Preventive

Photo credit: Pat Beekman.

Both domestic and feral cats are carriers of the Toxoplasma gondii single-celled parasite. Incredibly, the CDC states more than 60 million men, women, and children carry the Toxoplasma parasite.

Medicine, explained that cats are the *definitive* host of *Toxoplasma gondii*, the protozoan parasite that causes toxoplasmosis.

Toxoplasma reproduces only in cats, but can infect any warm-blooded mammal, including deer and humans. Cats release millions of eggs into the environment through their feces, where they remain infectious for up to eighteen months. Where domestic and feral cats occur, these infectious eggs are abundant and contaminate the environment. Deer pick up the eggs from the soil where deer and cats coexist.

Humans and Toxoplasma

Symptoms vary, but young children, pregnant women, and people with weakened immune systems are at greatest risk. Human infections have been linked to miscarriages, memory loss, and even death. According to Ballash, "Humans can become infected by consuming undercooked venison that contains toxoplasma tissue cysts." He added, "Consuming any meat product carries an inherent risk of getting a foodborne infection, and venison is no different. However, this should not deter individuals from consuming venison because cooking venison to the correct internal temperature and proper kitchen hygiene (washing contaminated surfaces and separating utensils used for meat from other foods) will allow safe consumption of venison, and meat in general."

The truth of the matter is that you and I and countless other deer hunters probably already have been infected with the *toxoplasma gandii* parasite. I have been eating rare-cooked venison for more than a half century and have not exhibited any of the signs of infection, as noted by the CDC. Hmmmm . . . But it's better to err on the side of caution than to remain ignorant about this disease. This is particularly true if you hunt suburban properties or in places with high numbers of feral cats. Then it is even more important to cook your tenderloin well done next time you fire up the grill. Yes, this is contrary to what almost everyone writes when discussing how to cook venison. But, if you are concerned about toxoplasmosis, then cooking venison to medium or medium-well is your best preventative option. **Otherwise, the Center for Disease Control says you can freeze venison for several days at sub-zero (0°F) temperatures before cooking to greatly reduce chance of infection.**

Photo credit: Canstock photo.

There is no documentation from any research I have done that can document how many deer carry Toxoplasmosis nationwide.

It is also important to note, however, that of the millions of men, women, and children in the US who carry the *Toxoplasma* parasite, very few have symptoms because the immune system usually keeps the parasite from causing illness.

To avoid toxoplasmosis, the CDC recommends cooking venison to at least 145°F for whole cuts of meat and 160°F for ground venison. The temperature should be measured by a food thermometer placed in the thickest part of the meat, then the meat should be allowed to rest for three minutes before carving.

CDC Recommended Tips:

- Freeze meat for several days at sub-zero (0°F) temperatures before cooking to greatly reduce chances of infection.
- Wash cutting boards, dishes, counters, utensils, and hands with hot soapy water after contact with raw meat, poultry, seafood, or unwashed fruits or vegetables.
- Wear gloves when gardening and during any contact with soil or sand because it might be contaminated with cat feces that contain *Toxoplasma*. Wash hands with soap and water after gardening or contact with soil or sand.
- Teach children the importance of washing hands to prevent infection.

So there you have it. I have advised you about *toxoplasmosis*. Hopefully, I didn't scare the poop out of you. The reality is, if you don't hunt areas with large populations of feral cats, you probably have very little to worry about concerning your chances of getting infected with toxoplasmosis. Therefore, you can get back to cooking your venison on the medium side (slightly pink in the middle) if you desire.

A Special Closing Note from the Author:

In several places in this book, I have mentioned a few products I use by their brand names. I don't include them to suggest in any way whatsoever that readers should purchase the brands I cited. I strongly believe the choice of buying products is solely up to the reader, and should not be swayed by any unintended influence.